Contents

ALL NEW 100 LITERACY HOURS: YEAR 1

About the series

The books in the updated *All New 100 Literacy Hours* series offer a set of completely new term-by-term lesson plans, complete with objectives and organisation grids and accompanied, where relevant, with photocopiable texts and activity sheets. The series offers a core of material for the teaching of the English curriculum within the structure of the Literacy Hour, but now perfectly matches the recent NLS *Medium-Term Plans*, *Grammar for Writing* and *Speaking, Listening, Learning* guidelines. The series also builds on current teaching ideas including providing activities to match children's preferred learning styles.

Using this book
The units of work

This book provides 100 Literacy Hours for Year 1 based on the *National Literacy Strategy Medium-Term Plans*, which either build to form a core scheme of work or which can be used to supplement your existing planning. This core should be extended in several ways. For example:
● Repeating the sequence of lessons, but with different texts, for example, Term 1, Narrative 2, could usefully be followed by a further traditional tale with a cumulative plot, for example 'The Gingerbread Man'.
● Adding additional texts, for example, Term 2, Non-fiction 1, is based on an early years non-fiction book which could usefully be doubled in length to exemplify a wider range of non-fiction book layouts.
● Giving extra time for the drafting and redrafting process. This is essential if it is to be done with the thoroughness recommended in NLS exemplification, for example: *Improving Writing: Writing Flier 1*.
● It is also well worth allowing more time for final presentation. An example is Term, Poetry 1, where the unit culminates in a reading aloud that can lead to a poetry event.
In addition to the above, tried-and-tested resources from previous schemes of work, other publications, or the original 100 Literacy Hours, can be used to supplement the new materials.

The lesson plans

The lesson plans should be seen as a source of ideas, not as a straitjacket, and should therefore be used flexibly. Most lessons plans can easily be adapted for rotational use by alternating the independent and guided activities. The number of guided activities that are possible in one week will depend on the number of available adults. When planning rotation, it is important to ensure that all children experience the key activities throughout the week. If following the linear model, guided activities will usually need to involve a guided version of the independent activity, otherwise children may miss out on key experiences.

INTRODUCTION

Organisation of teaching units

Each term is divided into teaching units comprising five or ten hours. Each of the units cluster the NLS text-, sentence- and word-level objectives. The units are organised as follows:

Unit overview

Introduction
Overview of each unit including ideas for extending units.

Organisation grid
Outlines the key activities for each lesson.

Key assessment opportunities
A bulleted list of key assessment opportunities. These will help you to plan assessment opportunities throughout each unit.

Unit lesson plans

Each unit of lesson plans is written with the following headings:

Objectives
NLS objectives including Speaking and listening emphases.

What you need
Provides a list of resources required for each lesson.

Shared work
Sets out the shared text-, sentence- and word-level work in each lesson. Some of these objectives are taught discretely, while others are integrated into the theme of the unit as the NLS recommends.

Guided work and Independent work
Every unit contains at least two suggestions for guided work to be used if the lessons plans are reorganised on a rotational basis. The lessons also include ideas for independent group, paired or individual activities. In some units, you may wish to re-organise these, along with the suggestions for guided work, on a rotational basis, for example, when a group set of books is being shared around the class.

Plenary
Sets out what to do in the whole-class plenary session.

Differentiation
Ideas for supporting or more or less able children including ideas for peer and other adult support.

Links to the NLS Medium-Term Plans

The units provide clear links to the requirements of the NLS *Medium-Term Plans*. Genres are matched exactly with appropriate texts for the age group and the range of objectives covered, as shown on the grid for each term. Some of the word- and sentence-level objectives identified in the *Medium-Term Plans* have been relocated from the specified units to meet the needs of specific texts and the running order of the selected units.

Differentiation

In every lesson plan, suggestions for supporting the less able and stretching the more able are given. However, it is important to use these advisedly as a child may be 'less able' in some aspects of literacy, but 'more able' in others. These suggestions should be applied when appropriate to the individual child and not be automatically given to a predetermined group. Other important considerations are children's different learning styles, and the concept of 'multiple intelligences'. Children also need to experience working individually, in pairs, and in a range of larger groups, organised in different ways to meet different educational objectives. The number of groups will depend on class size, spread of ability and learning style. Try to ensure a balance of gender and personality type in each group, and don't hesitate to separate children who cannot work well together.

Assessment

Each unit includes a list of bullet points to help with ongoing assessment. These are not intended to replace National Curriculum assessment, but represent the 'bottom line' that all the children should have achieved by the end of the unit. If a number of children have failed to achieve satisfactory standards in any of the bulleted areas, then the unit may need to be revisited (with different resources).

Using the photocopiable resources

Where there is instruction to copy material from copyright texts, you must ensure that this is done within the limits of the copying licence of your school. If pupils are using their own exercise books or paper for answers, then all photocopiable resources are reuseable.

Usually, the best way to share a resource with the class is to make a display version for an overhead projector or data projector. However, try to avoid this becoming routine. An effective alternative is to sit with the children in a circle and to work with a hard copy of the text and where possible, engage the children with actual books.

Interactive whiteboard use

Permission is granted for those pages marked as photocopiable to be used in this way. Where third party material is used, permission for interactive whiteboard use must be obtained from the copyright holder or their licensor. This information can be found in the acknowledgements at the front of the book.

Speaking and listening

When speaking and listening is one of the main focuses of the lessons, links are made to the Primary National Strategy's *Speaking, Listening and Learning* (DfES, 2003), and to the speaking and listening emphases within the *Medium-Term Planner*. These links are also highlighted in the objectives grid through the use of a logo .

Children will use speaking and listening as a process skill in every lesson. To encourage this, particular emphasis is given to children working with 'talk partners'. When a larger group is needed, 'talk partners' can join into fours. Groups of this size are ideal for discussion and collaborative work as they provide a range of opinion and yet are not too large to make full participation difficult. It is important to vary group organisation so that children experience working with different partners with different approaches or abilities.

Creativity

Recent reports have emphasised the importance of creativity and creativity is embedded within many of the lessons this book. Also encourage creativity by using some of the following ideas:
● Children as Real Writers - encourage children to see themselves as real writers writing for real purposes. This means giving them a strong sense of audience and purpose, using redrafting techniques and finding a way of 'publishing' completed work.
● Writing Journals - encourage the children to write something in their journal every day. This can be anything they like - diary entry, story, poem, exploration of a problem and so on. This is the one place where

grammar and punctuation do not matter. The aim is to develop writing fluency, that is, a free flow between thought and written page.

● First-Hand Experiences - many NLS writing tasks are responses to texts. Balance this by using stimulating 'real-life' starting points such as visits, visitors, artefacts, and so on.

● Experimentation - encourage the children to play with ideas and explore alternatives. Positively encourage them to suggest alternative tasks.

● Writing Materials – provide inspiring media such as paper in various colours and sizes; a variety of pens and pencils (for example, felt-tipped pens, calligraphic pens); rulers; scissors; glue; DTP and presentation software; a ClipArt library; a colour printer.

Learning styles

Researchers have identified three different learning styles: auditory, kinaesthetic and visual. Most children will use a mixture of all three styles, but in some children, one style will predominate. Many lessons in this book offer specific opportunities for different learning styles; however, it is useful to keep in mind at all times the needs of each learning style:

Visual learners
● learn by seeing and looking
● benefit from illustrations, diagrams and presentations
● are helped by visual text analysis techniques such as annotation.

Auditory learners
● learn by hearing and listening
● acquire knowledge by reading aloud, reciting and repeating
● are helped by clear verbal explanations and discussion.

Kinaesthetic learners
● learn by touching and doing
● rely on what they can directly experience or perform
● are helped by physically manipulating things.

Media and ICT

There have been major advances in media and ICT. For this reason, we need to give more emphasis to media education and ICT in the primary classroom. This can be done by showing film versions of books and documentaries on non-fiction topics. Most children are now able to access the internet at home, and most schools have internet access. In school, the data projector and interactive whiteboard are replacing the blackboard and OHT. It may seem challenging to integrate ICT into your literacy teaching. Think of simple ways to use it every day, for example, allowing children to use the internet and CD-ROMs for research, and ensuring that every time writing takes place, at least one group is using a word-processor.

NLS OBJECTIVES

Medium-term plan/ All New 100 Literacy Hours unit	Text level	Sentence level	Word level	Number of hours	Text(s)	Links to DEW, PiP Steps, S&L	Outcome
Narrative 1	T1 T5 T7 T8 T9 T11	S2 S4 S5 S8 S9	W1 W11	5	Going Shopping by Sarah Garland	DEW: p78. S&L: 3, 4	Storybooks about going shopping
Poetry 1	T1 T5 T8 T9 T11	S8	W7 W10 W11 W12	5	It Looked Like Spilt Milk by Charles G Shaw; Ketchup on your Cornflakes by Nick Sharratt	S&L: 1	Own picture books based on own experience and books read
Non-fiction 1	T8 T12 T15 T16	S2 S4	W8 W10 W12 W14	5	A shopping list by Kathleen Taylor	S&L: 3, 4	Role-play lists and instructions; timetable
Narrative 2	T1 T3 T4 T5 T7 T8 T9 T11	S3 S4 S5 S6 S8 S9	W4 W8 W9 W12 W14	10	The story of Chicken Licken' retold by Kathleen Taylor	DEW: p78. PIPs: Step 5. S&L: 1, 4	Oral retelling and role-play; mini books of own stories
Poetry 2	T4 T6 T7 T10	S2 S3	W1 W10	5	'Blow wind blow'; 'The north wind doth blow'	PIPs: Steps 4 and 5 S&L: 8, 9	Own rhymes; performance of rhymes
Non-fiction 2	T12 T13 T15 T16	S2 S4	W8 W10 W12	5	Picture recipes	S&L: 1, 2	Sandwich recipes; sandwiches

Medium-term plan/*All New 100 Literacy Hours* unit	Text level	Sentence level	Word level	Number of hours	Text(s)	Links to DEW, PiP Steps, S&L	Outcome
Narrative 1	T4 T6 T7 T8 T9 T10 T14 T15 T16	S4 S5 S7	W3 W10	10	'Mr Polar Bear and the Hobyahs' retold by Kathleen Taylor; 'The Greedy Guest' by Jane Grell	**DEW:** p78. **PiPs:** Steps 5–7. **S&L:** 5, 7, 8	Character portraits; role-play; new characters
Non-fiction 1	TT12 T17 T19 T20 T22 T23 T24 T25	S5 S6 S7	W10 W11	5	*A Seed in Need* by Sam Godwin	**S&L:** 6, 7	Class non-fiction Big Book
Poetry	T2 T11 T12 T13	S1	W1 W7 W10	5	'Chinese New Year' by Neela Mann; *One Smiling Grandma* by Anne Marie Linden	**PiPs:** Steps 4 and 5. **S&L:** 7, 9	Own poems inspired by those read
Narrative 2	T1 T4 T5 T8 T9 T10 T11 T20	S5 S7	W2 W3 W10	10	'The Imperial Nightingale' by Hans Christian Andersen; 'There was a princess long ago'	**DEW:** Unit 6, p78 **PiPs:** Step 5 **S&L:** 2, 5, 8	Retelling of story with puppets; performance of story in song and dance and on tape
Non-fiction 2	T18 T20 T21 T25	S2 S5	W5 W8 W10	5	*Caterpillars* by Barrie Watts		Class report on science topic

Medium-term plan/ *All New 100 Literacy Hours* unit	Text level	Sentence level	Word level	Number of hours	Text(s)	Links to DEW, PIP Steps, S&L	Outcome
Narrative 1 and 2	T2 T3 T5 T6 T7 T8 T10 T13 T14	S3 S6	W1 W3 W4 W5 W8 W10	10	'Patrick's class topic' by Kathleen Taylor; books such as *Q Pootle 5 in Space* by Nick Butterworth	**PIPs:** Step 7. **S&L:** 4, 9, 10, 11	3-D role-play; written and oral stories about fantasy worlds in space.
Poetry 1	T4 T9 T10 T11 T15 T16	S3	W8 W9	5	Let's do the flip-flop frolic' by Judith Nicholls; 'Sand' by John Foster	**PIPs:** Step 5. **S&L:** 9, 10	Own patterned poems; poetry reading
Non-fiction 1 and 2	T12 T17 T18 T19 T20 T21 T22	S5 S6 S7	W3, W6 W7 W8 W10	10	Photographs and objects collected from a visit	**DEW:** Unit 9. **S&L:** 7, 11	Class Big Book and group booklets recounting visit; 3-D display; information texts
Poetry 2	T2 T9 T11 T15 T16	S3 S6	W1 W5 W8	5	'Blast Off!'; 'Alien' by Kathleen Taylor	**PIPs:** Step 7. **S&L:** 7, 9, 12	Poetic sentences for reading aloud and describing own paintings

UNIT 1

Narrative 1

This unit is based around the familiar setting of shops and supermarkets. Children compose individual and collaborative storybooks that show them drawing from their own experiences of going shopping. *Going Shopping* by Sarah Garland (Puffin) is used as a model for writing. Guided and independent work is designed as a continuum rather than isolated activities in order to strengthen children's understanding of the writing process. Hours 3 and 4 link to 'Developing the concept of a sentence' in *Developing Early Writing*. This unit also relates to Unit 4 in *Developing Early Writing*.

Hour	Shared text-level work	Shared word-/ sentence-level work	Guided work	Independent work	Plenary
1 Reading the story	Reading the story and relating it to own experiences.	Exploring rhyming strings.	Re-reading; recognising high-frequency words; developing comprehension.	Beginning a story about going shopping.	Discussing how the children planned their story.
2 Reading the pictures	Reading the messages conveyed in the pictures, focusing on characterisation.	Reinforcing skills for reading and writing new words.	Interpreting illustrations to aid reading for meaning.	Interpreting the story through drama.	Discussing how drama can deepen children's understanding of a story.
3 Demonstrating writing	Shared writing of story sentences.	Shared writing of story sentences.	Practising strategies for writing.	Continuing writing individual or collaborative storybook.	Modelling writing for each other.
4 Features of books	Exploring storybook text conventions and cover features.	Demarcating sentences; revising spelling strategies.	Practising strategies for writing.	Assembling their stories in sequence to compile a book.	Sharing individual stories; discussing plans.
5 Making a cover	Discussing similarities and differences in the children's stories.	Identifying features of a sentence.	Writing titles for the children's books.	Making front covers; completing the books.	Reading and commenting on each other's books; displaying the books in the classroom.

Key assessment opportunities
● Have the children drawn upon their own experiences to convey a story?
● Can they write sentences that make sense?
● Can they use capital letters and full stops appropriately?

Reading the story

Objectives

NLS
T5: To describe story settings and incidents and relate them to own experience.
S4: To write captions and simple sentences.
W1: To practise and secure the ability to rhyme, and to relate this to spelling patterns through generating rhyming strings.

S&L
4 Drama: To describe incidents or tell stories from their own experience, in an audible voice.

What you need
● Copies of *Going Shopping* by Sarah Garland (Puffin)
● Photocopiable pages 17-19.

Shared text-level work
● Read *Going Shopping*. The story is held in the pictures at least as much as the text so it is essential that some interpretation is shared with the children. However, the next shared session will devote more time to this.
● Encourage the children to make connections between the story and their real-life experiences of going shopping. What similarities and differences can they see?
● Ask questions that encourage the children to talk about their experiences, for example:

> ● Do you go in a car? Or do you walk or catch a bus?
> ● Do you go to local shops or travel to a supermarket?
> ● Who goes on the shopping trip?
> ● What do you buy?

● Ask the children to discuss their shopping trips with their partners.

Shared word- and sentence-level work
● Write the word *shop* on the board and ask the children to think of words that rhyme with it, for example *chop, mop, stop*. Talk about the spelling pattern *op*.
● Now change the *o* to *e* and think of words like *step*. Not many words end in *ep* so allow the children to invent words, but move on quickly to *ip, up* and *ap* spellings, again asking the children to suggest words.

Guided work
● Re-read *Going Shopping* together and then ask the children to read it independently. Check if the children can recognise the high-frequency words on sight.
● Ask further questions that enable the children to interpret the pictures and make connections between the story and their own experiences of going shopping.

Independent work
● Organise the children to work with their talk partners. Tell them that they are going to make a book similar to *Going Shopping*, but it will be their own story.
● Give each child photocopiable page 18. Explain that they should use the sheet to draw a sequence of pictures about when they go shopping, drawing one picture in each box. Underneath each box, they can write a short sentence about what is happening in the picture. Explain that they will have an opportunity to write more later.

Differentiation

Less able
● Give the children a selection of word cards from photocopiable page 19 to help them write the first page of their book.

More able
● Help the children to plan a collaborative story on large sheets of paper.

Plenary
● Ask the more able group how they made decisions about what to include in their story. What gave them their ideas? Did they use their explanations of the pictures in the book to help them plan their story?

UNIT 1 HOUR 2 — Narrative 1

Reading the pictures

Objectives

NLS
T1: To reinforce and apply their word-level skills.
T7: To re-enact stories.
S2: To use awareness of the grammar of a sentence to decipher new or unfamiliar words.

S&L
4 Drama: To explore familiar themes and characters through improvisation and role-play.

What you need
● *Going Shopping* by Sarah Garland (Puffin)
● photocopiable page 17.

Differentiation

Less able
● Provide plastic mirrors and a floor-standing mirror. Tell children to practise facial expressions and gestures.

More able
● Encourage the children to convey their characters feelings through facial expression and gesture. Intervene when timely so that children can reflect and comment on how well they are capturing the scene.

Shared text-level work
● In this session you are going to concentrate on reading the inference in the pictures, rather than the previous focus on what was happening in the text.
● You will need to form questions to help the children describe how the characters are feeling. Consider, for example, the expressions on the characters' faces.
● Relate this to the children's own experiences of shopping: the sorts of things that happen, the things they see and how they and others feel. Encourage the children to provide examples from their plans.

Shared sentence-level work
● Show *In you go* from the book and choose a child to read the sentence. Ask the children if they have noticed *go* in another word (*going* from the title).
● Display other sentences for the children to read. Recall the strategies the children could use in reading, such as *Guess what comes next,* (grammatical awareness), *Know the word by sight, Use initial sound or letter to help predict the whole word.*

Guided work
● Continue as Hour 1, with two groups spending about ten minutes each with the classroom assistant.
● Concentrate on reading the inference conveyed in the pictures. Use photocopiable page 17 to help form questions so that the children can explore the characters' feelings and relationships.

Independent work
● Arrange the classroom to leave a large space for drama work, and organise the children into groups of four.
● Allocate each group a different sequence of pictures from *Going Shopping* and tell the children they are to provide their own dramatised version of that part of the story. Advise them to think about who will be the adults, children and dog, what they might be feeling, doing and saying.
● At an appropriate time, stop the children and choose a group to act their scene. Use this to refocus the children's attention on making use of expression and gesture to convey meaning as well as using dialogue.

Plenary
● View the other groups' scenes from *Going Shopping.*
● Bring the session to a close by asking children to suggest what more have they learned about the story through their re-enactments.
● Ask the children: *How do you think Mum was feeling at the checkouts? How was she feeling on her way home? Do you think baby enjoyed going shopping? Which bits did baby enjoy most and how can you tell? What about the dog? How do you think it felt when the others went into the supermarket?*

UNIT 1 HOUR 3 ▭ Narrative 1

Demonstrating writing

Objectives

NLS

T8: Through shared and guided writing to apply phonological, graphic knowledge and sight vocabulary to spell words accurately.
T9: To write about events in personal experience linked to a variety of familiar incidents from stories.
S4: To write captions and simple sentences, and to re-read, recognising whether or not they make sense.
W11: To spell common irregular words from Appendix List 1.

What you need

● Completed planning sheets from photocopiable page 18
● word cards from photocopiable page 19
● the children's stories so far
● sheets of A5 paper.

Differentiation

Less able
● Provide appropriate word cards from photocopiable page 18.

More able
● Continue as Hour 1. Organise the children in pairs and give one pair responsibility for how the story begins, another for what happens when they get to the shop and another for doing the shopping.

Shared work

● This session covers text- and sentence-level objectives in a holistic shared lesson.
● Tell the children that you are going to help them write their shopping stories and begin by choosing a child who can start the story off.
● The child might choose the opening phrase *In we go*, so ask questions to extend it. You may find a child provides a whole sentence, for example *Mum fastens Joe in his seat but I can fasten my own seatbelt.*
● Count the number of words the child contributes, then begin to write, encouraging the children to show their understanding of sentence structure and spelling. For example, begin with a lower-case letter so that children can correct you; keep asking if the developing sentence sounds right – are there any 'better' words that could be used or words you might change around?
● Encourage the children to draw upon their knowledge of spelling patterns and words within words as you work.
● When you reach the end of the sentence, don't add a full stop and wait for the children to correct you and explain why this is wrong.
● Conclude the session by asking volunteers to explain some of the strategies used in composing the sentence.

Guided work

● Continue to demonstrate the strategies for writing as in the shared session with small groups of children.
● Give the children word cards from photocopiable page 19 to help with their writing.
● Engage the children in the writing process by rehearsing a sentence orally. Ask questions to enable the children to structure their sentences around their shopping experiences.
● Concentrate on letter formation for those children who need extra practice in this.

Independent work

● Ensure that the children have their planning sheets and additional A5 paper, which will form pages for their storybooks.
● Ask the children to continue to compose their story, writing simple sentences and drawing detailed illustrations.

Plenary

● Choose a sentence that a child has written and ask the child to read it aloud.
● Now ask another child to be 'teacher' and demonstrate at the board (with help from you and the other children) how to write the sentence.
● Involve the other children in the process, particularly those who you wish to assess for understanding of spelling strategies, knowledge of irregular spellings and appropriate use of capital letters and full stops.

Features of books

Objectives

NLS

T11: To make simple picture storybooks with sentences, modelling them on basic text conventions.
S8: To begin using full stops to demarcate sentences.
S9: To use a capital letter for the start of a sentence.

S&L

3 Group discussion and interaction: To ask and answer questions, make relevant contributions, offer suggestions and take turns.

What you need

● *Going Shopping* by Sarah Garland (Puffin)
● completed planning sheet photocopiable page 18
● photocopiable page 19
● the children's stories so far
● sugar-paper books to contain the stories.

Differentiation

Less able

● Let children draw and write any further pages to complete their story, using word cards from photocopiable 19 for support.

More able

● Ask the group to complete their writing, read it together and assemble it in the appropriate sequence in the collaborative book, leaving suitable space for illustrations.

Shared text-level work

● Display *Going Shopping* and look carefully at the layout. Identify the title, author, picture and publisher's logo.
● Then discuss the layout of the introductory pages:
1. the title
2. a picture of the family actually going shopping
3. then words and pictures together giving the author's name, the title, the publisher and a picture (which indicates there is more to the story than just going shopping).
● Continue to turn the pages, discussing the layout as you read. Notice, for example, that the writing is at the top of the page. Affirm the need for the children to think about how they will arrange text and pictures in their own books.

Shared sentence-level work

● Display two sentences written by children of similar ability level and ask how we know they are sentences. (Both have capital letters at the start and full stops at the end.)
● Ask the two writers what strategies they used to spell difficult words and write their strategies on the board to serve as a reminder of what to do when writing a new word.

Guided work

● Continue from previous lessons, ensuring the children can refer to reminders of spelling strategies.
● Organise the children to work in pairs so that they can help one another put their story scenes in the right order in their books and help each other to write.

Independent work

● Ensure that the children have their planning sheets and writing, together with blank books in which to stick the pages of their stories.
● Tell them to cut out and stick their pictures and writing into the pages of the blank book to make their story book.
● Before they cut anything out, encourage them to discuss their story with their partners and to work out together the appropriate order in which to stick down the pictures and writing.
● Remind the children about the layout features you discussed in shared work.

Plenary

● Organise the children to sit in a horseshoe shape. Place the higher ability group in the gap at the top of the horseshoe and prepare them to read out sections of their story.
● Following the reading, discuss how they might develop the pictures to enhance the story.
● Ask the children to turn to their partners to discuss how to develop their stories further. Ask a couple of children to explain their intentions.

TERM 1

Making a cover

Objectives

NLS

T11: To make simple picture storybooks with sentences, modelling them on basic text conventions, e.g. cover, author's name, title, layout.
S5: To recognise full stops and capital letters when reading, and name them correctly.

What you need
● The children's story books
● cartridge paper to make covers
● art and craft materials
● a selection of picture books in plastic wallets.

Shared text-level work
● This session highlights the individuality and originality of the children's stories whilst recognising similarities in terms of writing conventions. Choose two children's stories that are different in content, for example local shop/supermarket, bus/car, but similar in level.
● Praise all of the children for their stories and read the chosen two. Question the authors about the differences: *What do you like about your local shop? What do you like about your supermarket? What are the difficulties? What are the benefits?*
● Ask all of the children to turn to their partners, tell each other their story and discuss differences and similarities.
● Ask how their story's content might influence the cover picture. For example, *James, you travel on the bus to the supermarket and have to help Mum to carry lots of bags home on the bus. What will you include in your cover picture?* Allow the child to answer, then ask him to think of a title for his story. Do this using another child's story.
● Recall cover features identified previously: picture, title, author, publisher and how the picture and title reflect the story.

Shared sentence-level work
● Read enlarged versions of one sentence from each of the two children's stories. Ask if there are any similarities.
● Pose questions so that the children recognise that, for example, both sentences make sense, they go beyond the end of the line, capital letters and full stops demarcate beginnings and endings.

Guided work
● Work with two groups to write titles for their books.

Independent work
● Ask the children to finish their stories and produce front covers for their books.
● Provide a selection of picture books to look at as a visual reference. (Seal them in plastic wallets so that the children can't be distracted by the story inside.)

Differentiation

Less able
● Work with this group to support them in making front covers and choosing appropriate materials and colours.

More able
● Ask the children to work together to make the front cover for their collaborative book including a 'logo' of their own design, discussing the positions and styles of the different features as well as the content.

Plenary
● Tell the children to ensure their work is neatly arranged on their table because they are going to swap tables and look at the work of other children. Stress to the children that they must take great care of other people's work as they read it and look at the pictures.
● Conclude the plenary by asking two or three children to say what they like about the book they are looking at. Ask how well the front cover captures what is inside.
● Draw attention to any logos and ask the children to give reasons for their designs.
● Provide further opportunities for children to share their work by placing finished books on a library shelf or wall display rack.

Inference in pictures

Teacher's note: *This prompt sheet can be used by the Classroom Assistant in preparation for talking to children about the story conveyed in the pictures.*

Encourage the children to gain understanding of the story by talking about what is happening in the pictures. Ask questions that explore the relationship between the characters and what they are thinking and feeling and relate to the children's own experiences. Listed below are some points to note.

Pre-title page: everyone is eager to go shopping; only baby has spotted blackbird (they are looking at each other); dog is following little girl.

Title page: game of hide and seek between dog and girl; the expression on their faces is indicative of a special relationship.

Pages 1 and 2: concentration of girl fastening seat belt; dog looking across at little girl, another indication of their special relationship.

Pages 3 and 4: dog leaping eagerly into car; girl's eyes looking over seat to check that dog is safely in the car; neighbour in garden looking on.

Pages 5 and 6: cat in tree trying to catch bird; dogs waiting at foot of tree for cat; man reading map in car; another mum with baby, possibly returning from shopping (a different experience of shopping to that of the main family).

Pages 7 and 8: dog joining in with girl reading book; mum's expression of confidence whilst driving.

Pages 9 and 10: girl's anxious expression as she feels for the ground as she gets out of the car; expression of affection between mum and baby.

Pages 11 and 12: dog's sad expression as he is tied up outside the supermarket; eagerness of girl to go shopping; baby looking back sympathetically at the dog.

Pages 13 and 14: concentrating on shopping.

Pages 15 and 16: two babies noticing each other; parents meanwhile are busy concentrating on shopping.

Pages 17 and 18: baby asleep; serious adult faces around checkouts.

Pages 19 and 20: mum's tired expression as she carries everything for everybody and, of course, baby; dog doesn't want to go now.

Pages 21 and 22: everyone's tired and ready for home.

Pages 23 and 24: girl reading to baby whose head is on one side, taking an interest in the book.

Pages 25 and 26: mum looking quite shattered; dog's tongue hanging out – ready for a drink; girl helping to carry happy baby; blackbird sitting other way on nest, watching their return; again only baby notices the blackbird.

Planning your story

◼ Draw your own sequence of pictures about when you go shopping. ◼
◼ Write a sentence below each picture.

Word cards

car	bus	seat belt
road	car park	money
trolley	drinks	food
till	pay	home
tired	list	bags

UNIT 2

Poetry 1

This five-hour unit is based on two simple picture books, *It Looked Like Spilt Milk* by Charles G Shaw (HarperCollins) and *Ketchup On Your Cornflakes?* by Nick Sharratt (Scholastic Hippo). Both texts use patterned language to explore everyday things through a child's eye, where the usual becomes the unusual, providing thought-provoking and often funny outcomes. The books provide a basis from which children can create their own books for the class library. Hour 5 links to *Progression in Phonics* Step 7.

Hour	Shared text-level work	Shared word-/sentence-level work	Guided work	Independent work	Plenary
1 Can you guess what it is?	Reading *It Looked Like Spilt Milk*; discussing own experiences.	Talking about descriptions and explanations, using *because*.	Re-reading, focusing on images created.	Discussing cloud shapes observed outdoors.	Sharing their experiences of watching clouds.
2 Modelling writing	Using the refrain from the book to begin own writing; practising spelling and writing sentences.	Using the refrain from the book to begin own writing; practising spelling and writing sentences.	Writing sentences related to own experiences.	Beginning an illustrated book based on *It Looked Like Spilt Milk*.	Sharing their books; discussing what to do next.
3 Titles and endings	Reading one of the children's books; discussing ideas for the title page and ending.	Scribing an ending for the story, reinforcing the concept of a sentence.	Writing sentences related to own experiences; disussing ideas for the title page and ending.	Constructing a title page and ending.	Celebrating the children's work; discussing spelling strategies.
4 Ketchup On Your Cornflakes?	Reading *Ketchup On Your Cornflakes?*; experimenting with different sentence combinations.	Using prepositions incorrectly so children begin to recognise them.	Using the book to develop sight-recognition of prepositions.	Making picture storybooks similar to *Ketchup On Your Cornflakes?*	Refocusing on the purpose of writing books for the library; discussing next steps.
5 Celebration of class library	Re-reading, continuing to check prepositions; reading one of the children's books.	Explore spelling patterns especially graphic–phonic correspondence and words within words.	Revising how to use the library.	Completing their books with a cover.	Celebrating the children's achievements and how their books are part of the class library; discussing spelling strategies.

Key assessment opportunities
● Can the children read and recite poems, paying attention to punctuation and rhyme?
● Have they used simple poetry structures to write their own poems?
● Do they use phonological and graphical knowledge to spell words?
● Do they understand that words with the same sounds may be spelled differently?
● Is their knowledge of long-vowel digraphs secure?

Can you guess what it is?

Objectives

NLS
T5: To describe story settings and incidents and relate them to own experience and that of others.
W7: To read on sight high-frequency words.

S&L
1 Speaking: To describe incidents from their own experience, in an audible voice.

What you need
● *It Looked Like Spilt Milk* by Charles G Shaw (HarperCollins)
● clipboards
● digital camera(s).

Differentiation

Less able
● Give children appropriate verbal scaffolding to help them articulate and share their ideas.

More able
● Work with this group using digital cameras to capture a variety of cloud formations for discussion.

Shared text-level work
● Read the first three pages of *It Looked Like Spilt Milk*, up to *Sometimes it looked like a bird*, ensuring that the children see the text and pictures.
● Ask the children if they can guess what *it* is.
● Continue to read in order to find out. Keep asking the children to guess in order to build up their sense of anticipation. The predictable repeating frame should allow the children to read with confidence.
● On the last page, show surprise as you notice the additional text (*It was just a cloud in the sky*), but before reading it say, *I wonder what this says* and *I wonder if our guesses were right.* Then read the line and enjoy solving the mystery with the children.
● Relate the story to the children's experiences by asking if they have ever looked at a cloud and been reminded of something.
● Suggest that as they have so many super ideas perhaps they could write a book like *Spilt Milk*, but with their own pictures and descriptions.

Shared word-level work
● Explain that often what one person can see, another can't, therefore it is important to be able to *describe* what they see to help others see it.
● Turn to the page in the book where the cloud is like a sheep and ask the children why it looks like a sheep. Write *because* on the board and explain how this word can begin their explanation. Share ideas.

Guided work
● Re-read the book, encouraging the children to use reading strategies for new words. Also provide time for them to read the book independently.
● Emphasise the way in which the book establishes the images the cloud shapes conjure.

Independent work
● Organise the children into talk pairs and take them outside where they can sit together to watch and talk about different cloud shapes.
● Provide each pair with a clipboard so that they can draw and write their ideas. A drawing and/or one word each time is sufficient as the main objective is for children to collect lots of ideas. Tell them to collect as many ideas as they can for making a shared book with their partners.

Plenary
● Stay outdoors. Arrange the children into mixed-ability groups of four to explore and explain their various ideas and forms of work.
● Conclude by choosing a pair to share their ideas with the class. Focus on the way in which the word *because* helped them to begin their explanation.

Modelling writing

Objectives

NLS
T8: To apply phonological, graphic knowledge and sight vocabulary to spell words accurately.
T9: To write about events from personal experience linked to familiar incidents from stories.
T11: To make simple picture storybooks with sentences, modelling them on basic text conventions.
S8: To begin using full stops to demarcate sentences.
W11: To spell common irregular words from Appendix List 1.

What you need

● Blank books (the number of pages depending on ability)
● sticky notes
● a date stamp.

Shared work

● In this session, text, word and sentence objectives are met in a holistic way.
● Before the lesson, set up a role-play library in the classroom with sticky notes and a date stamp. Children will use the library to borrow books later in the unit.
● Remind the children about the shared 'cloud' books they are going to make.
● Alert them to the library area as a place where they will keep their finished books so that others can read them.
● Write the refrain from the book, *Sometimes it looked like a...* on the board, emphasising correct letter formation and encouraging the children to suggest spellings.
● Choose a pair of children to provide an idea from a photograph they took in Hour 1, for example *dinosaur* and add this to the refrain.
● Discuss continuing the sentence/rhyme with the word *because*.
● Explain why there is no need for a full stop at this point and go on to add the children's descriptive explanation of the cloud. For example, *Sometimes it looked like a dinosaur because it had a huge body and a long tail.*
● Use capital letters and a full stop appropriately.
● Cover the sentence and choose children to attempt to spell some of the high-frequency words used.
● Praise the children for knowing how to spell words and reassure them of the skills they have for writing their own books.

Guided work

● Model and demonstrate writing sentences for a rhyme by scribing children's ideas related to their first-hand experience of observing clouds.

Independent work

● Organise children to work in the same pairs as Hour 1.
● Provide blank books and tell the children to set out their books in the same way as *It Looked Like Spilt Milk* – with writing on one page and a picture on another.
● Drawings from the previous session could be stuck into the book rather than drawing them again.
● The main task is for children to construct their rhyme sentences in the same way as you did using the refrain *Sometimes it looked like a... because...* The children should take turns at being scribe and talk about content, spellings and letter formation.

Differentiation

Less able
● Encourage the children to describe the shapes in their pictures. Ask them to stick their pictures on alternate pages and support their writing.

More able
● Children should use their photographs to construct their books. Encourage correct sentence punctuation and suitable layout for the rhyme.

Plenary

● As in Hour 1, organise the children into mixed-ability groups of four to share their books.
● Ask the children what they have to do next in order to complete their books, for example add a cover or an ending.

Titles and endings

Objectives

NLS
T1: To reinforce and apply their word-level skills through shared and guided reading.
T11: To make simple picture storybooks with sentences, modelling them on basic text conventions.
S8: To begin using full stops to demarcate sentences.

What you need

● A wall display of cloud photographs taken in Hour 1
● one of the children's cloud books, enlarged.

Differentiation

Less able
● Ask the children to help you complete the wall display by suggesting captions to accompany the photographs. You should scribe, but encourage the children to help you with spellings.

More able
● Challenge the children to think of more than one ending to give a different 'twist' to their story.

Shared text-level work

● Prior to this session prepare a wall display using large photographs of clouds taken in Hour 1. If possible use the library area for the display.
● Write in large print above the photographs the refrain *Sometimes it looked like…*
● Draw the children's attention to the wall display and briefly explain that a group is going to help you write suggestions for what the clouds look like.
● Organise the children to sit with their talk partners. Display the first double-page of one of the children's books.
● Tell the class whose book it is and ask the pair of authors to read out their text.
● Organise for them to take turns at pointing and reading until the entire book has been read.
● Then ask everyone for ideas for a title page and ask them to suggest a layout and a suitable picture.
● Tell the children that an ending to the story is also needed. Ask the pairs to discuss how the book might end. They may suggest an ending similar to the book, for example *but it was just a cloud in the sky,* but be prepared to use their own endings as well.

Shared sentence-level work

● Emphasise correct letter formation as you scribe a suggested ending and involve children in spelling words.
● Reinforce the term *sentence* and correct use of capital letters and full stops.
● Return to the children's book to relate the suggested ending to the whole text.

Guided work

● Model the writing process by scribing children's ideas related to their firsthand experience of observing clouds and their ideas for the title page and ending of their books.

Independent work

● Organise the children in their pairs to collaborate in constructing a title page and ending for their own book as modelled in the shared session.

Plenary

● Celebrate the children's achievements. Organise for mixed groups to share their books and discuss the wall display.
● Refer to the wall display and select children who worked with you to talk about some of the spelling strategies they used.
● Conclude the session by letting the children place their books on shelves in the class library. Encourage them to look at other children's work but remind them to handle the books carefully.

UNIT 2 HOUR 4 Poetry 1

Curious combinations

Objectives
T11: To make simple picture storybooks with sentences, modelling them on basic text conventions.
W7: To read on sight high-frequency words.
W10: To recognise the critical features of words, e.g. words within words.

What you need
● *Ketchup On Your Cornflakes?* by Nick Sharratt (Scholastic Hippo)
● envelopes containing preposition cards *on, in, up, down, over*
● blank eight- or four-page books based on the format of *Ketchup on Your Cornflakes?* – with split pages so that different tops and bottoms can be combined
● photocopiable page 26.

Shared text-level work
● Introduce the book and read some of the highly amusing combinations, but then involve the children in learning how to use the sectioned pages of the book to create even more hilarious combinations.
● Discuss how the layout of the book provides lots of opportunity for variety. Also talk about how the pictures assist reading.

Shared word-level work
● Show the children how changing a 'little' word can make further funny combinations. Do this by reading some of the phrases incorrectly, for example *Custard **down** your…* instead of *Custard **on** your…* Children will realise the need to concentrate on the words in order to catch you out.
● Write the prepositions from the cards on the board, so that children can see how they are spelt.
● Then write the word *your* and ask the children to name the letters. Talk about the need to remember the spelling of this word because it isn't a word that you can sound out.
● Ask the children if they can see another word inside *your* (*our*) and invite a couple of children to write the words on the board from memory.
● Tell the children that they are going to make their own books similar to *Ketchup On Your Cornflakes?* for the class library.

Guided work
● Using *Ketchup On Your Cornflakes?*, continue to play at using prepositions incorrectly so that children become more able to recognise them on sight.

Independent work
● Organise the children to work with talk partners. Provide each pair with an envelope of prepositions together with a blank book. Ask the children to use the word cards to create a collaborative book.
● Ask them to use drawings similar to Nick Sharratt's book but to attempt to write the word too if they can.
● Ensure that the children take turns at writing an idea; they should each try to write two ideas for the book.

Plenary
● Seat the children facing the class library. Tell the children how excited you are about the new books they are creating that can be added to the library.
● Select children from each group to read their work so far.
● Use the last few minutes to discuss the next steps in creating their books.
● Tell the children that they should now be thinking of a title and cover picture for their book.

Differentiation

Less able
● Provide photocopiable page 26 for children to cut out and use the pictures and labels in their book according to the idea they want to create.

More able
● Children should work individually to create their own book. Encourage them to illustrate their ideas.

Celebrating the class library

Objectives

NLS

T8: Through shared and guided writing to apply phonological, graphic knowledge and sight vocabulary to spell words accurately.

T11: To make simple picture storybooks with sentences, modelling them on basic text conventions, e.g. cover, title, layout.

W12: To learn new words from reading and shared experiences, and to make collections of personal interest or significant words and words linked to particular topics.

What you need

● *Ketchup On Your Cornflakes?* by Nick Sharrat (Scholastic Hippo)
● an enlarged copy of one of the children's books made in Hour 4
● photocopiable page 26.

Differentiation

Less able
● Provide support to promote discussion about the title and cover for their books.

More able
● Ask the children to complete their books, then make a collection on a separate piece of paper of all the new words they have used.

Shared text-level work

● Read *Ketchup on Your Cornflakes?*, encouraging the children to join in. Misread *on* for *in*, and *in* for *on* and so on, so that the children have to correct you.
● Ask the children if they are having fun making their own books. Display a child's book, requesting another child to read it.
● Explore what happens when the page parts are mixed and matched, and have fun reading the combinations with the children.
● Return to the original book and talk about the front cover and title. Ask the children what their choice of title would be for their books. Would it be their favourite and funniest combination of pages?

Shared word-level work

● Focus on the words the children have been using in their books, such as *ketchup, custard, gravy,* and ask the children how they worked out the spellings. *Ketchup* is phonically regular and can be sounded out. Tell the children to listen to the sound you make from the three letters (trigraph) *tch*.
● Ask the children if they can think of any other words where they have heard this sound, for example *match, fetch, pitch, catch, latch, thatch, batch*. Write these on the board so that the children can see the spelling pattern. While *u* and *p* represent a sound–letter correspondence, they are much better remembered as the whole word that they make – *up*.

Guided work

● Work with one group to establish procedures for using the library including using the date stamp and keeping a file of children borrowing books.
● Prepare the group to role-play the process of using the library in the plenary so that other children in the class know how to borrow the newly made books.

Independent work

● Ask the pairs to work together to complete their books by providing a title and cover. Provide photocopiable page 26 for children who may want to use some of the pictures in their books or as a means of checking spellings.

Plenary

● Celebrate the children's achievements and the development of the class library, which now has lots of the children's own books for others to enjoy.
● Ask the higher ability group to share their list of words. Focus on spelling strategies by asking them to explain how they overcame difficulties.
● Conclude the session by asking the group to role-play how the class library is used.

TERM 1

Food mix and match

ketchup	milk	lemonade	jam
custard	pizza	yoghurt	fish fingers
ice-cream	sausages	crisps	cornflakes
gravy	mustard	sandwiches	chips

UNIT 3 ▭

Non-fiction 1

The main purpose of this five-hour unit is to create a supermarket in order to promote a sense of autonomy within the classroom and encourage the children's ownership of their surroundings. It will also provide a purposeful context for speaking and listening, reading and writing. The supermarket will enable the children to act out imaginary and real-life scenarios in a familiar setting and link to the unit 'Narrative 1' (page 11). Other curricular links should be made, such as maths (money) and ICT (Internet shopping).

Hour	Shared text-level work	Shared word-/ sentence-level work	Guided work	Independent work	Plenary
1 Making a supermarket	Collecting key words for supermarket topic.	Collecting key words for supermarket topic.	Matching grocery items to name labels.	Listing items for the class supermarket.	Assembling items in the class supermarket; deciding what labels to use.
2 💬 Using the supermarket	Reading part 1 of a story about shopping; discussing own experiences.	Promoting spelling strategies for new words.	Reading key words from the topic; practising spelling.	Sorting items according to department.	Discussing spelling strategies and choices for organising items.
3 💬 Using the supermarket	Explain how to use the supermarket; discussing lists and instructions.	Explain how to use the supermarket; discussing lists and instructions.	Writing sets of instructions.	Writing and drawing simple instructions as a booklet.	Comparing each other's instructions.
4 Internet shopping	Reading part 2 of the story to set the context for learning about online shopping.	Recognising sight words; using spelling strategies to recognise less familiar words.	Re-reading the whole story.	Showing understanding of internet shopping; using computer to order goods.	Using the role-play supermarket to verify ordering processes.
5 💬 Making a timetable	Planning a timetable; reading the days of the week.	Reading each other's names; practising letter formation.	Completing the timetable.	Showing understanding of how to organise deliveries; reading the timetable. Reading online order forms and delivering goods; matching words to pictures.	Describing processes and explaining how problems were overcome.

Key assessment opportunities

● Can the children discuss their experiences of shopping?

● Can they write simple instructions?

● Can they use a range of strategies for spelling new words?

● Are they forming letters correctly?

▭ 27

UNIT 3 HOUR 1 ◗ Non-fiction 1

Making a supermarket

Objectives

NLS

T8: Through guided reading apply phonological and graphic knowledge to spell words accurately.
T16: To write labels for everyday classroom use, e.g. in role-play area.
W12: To make collections of words from shared experiences and words linked to particular topics.

What you need

● Supermarket role-play area, including two rows of tables as aisles, and a checkout
● pretend and real goods to stock, such as fizzy drinks, shampoo, vegetables, cereal boxes
● aisle labels, such as *hair care, cereals, fruit and vegetables, bread*
● carrier bags or boxes.

Differentiation

Less able
● Children should work in pairs, each with a bag of mixed items to match to appropriate labels in the same way as the shared session.

More able
● Ask each pair to write what they think the labels should be for the groups of items that the other children have at their tables.

Shared text- and word-level work

● In this session, text and word objectives are met in a holistic way.
● Tell the children about your idea for having a supermarket in the classroom.
● Take the children on a 'tour' of the supermarket role-play area, explaining the function of the different parts such as the aisles and the checkout.
● Collect suggestions on the board of what the children would like to sell in their supermarket. Encourage the children to think about any trips they have made to the supermarket and the types of foods that they saw.
● As you write down children's suggestions, involve them in the spellings as far as possible, pointing out significant spelling patterns as in *peas, beans, meat,* and similar beginnings of words, such as *cheese, chicken, chocolate, chips,* and words within words: *washing-up liquid, washing powder.*
● Talk about how the items would be grouped in the supermarket.
● Provide items such as a bottle of shampoo, a can of fizzy drink and a tin of beans with the corresponding labels *hair care, drinks, tinned food.*
● Ask the children to match the items to the labels and explain their choices.

Guided work

● Provide a carrier bag containing specific items, for example a banana, a cereal packet, a bread roll and a can of fizzy drink.
● Spread labels on the table: *fruit and vegetables, cereals, bread, cheese, drinks,* and ask a child to pick an item from the bag and pick up and read out the correct label.

Independent work

● Provide a bag or box of items that have already been grouped.
● Tell the children that in order to stock the shop, lists of every item on sale need to be made. Their task is to make a list of all the items in their bag.
● Provide additional bags to unpack for those who complete the task before others.

Plenary

● Organise for each group, with the support of the classroom assistant, to place their items on the tables in the supermarket and pin their accompanying list to the wall directly behind.
● Then discuss the lists of labels from the more able group. Be prepared to distinguish between similar labels such as *cleaning goods* or *washing up, bread* or *bakery.*
● Make decisions with the children about the labels they want to choose for their supermarket.
● Choose one or two labels to reinforce spellings of key words.

Using the supermarket 1

Objectives

NLS

S2: To use awareness of grammar to decipher new or unfamiliar words.
T8: Through shared and guided reading to apply phonological, graphic knowledge and sight vocabulary to spell words accurately.
W10: To recognise the critical features of words, e.g. common spelling patterns and words within words.

S&L

4 Drama: To explore familiar themes and characters through improvisation and role-play.

What you need

● Photocopiable pages 33 and 35
● an enlarged copy of the shopping list from photocopiable page 33
● role-play items, including shopping baskets and a till.

Differentiation

Less able

● Let children use the supermarket. Provide support so that children can be familiarised with different roles: checkout assistant, shelf-stacker, customer.
● After ten minutes, swap with a more able group and provide a simplified version of the photocopiable sheet.

More able

● Ask the children to work in pairs to write shopping lists to use when role-playing in the supermarket.

Shared text-level work

● Before the lesson, use maths sessions to prepare price tags for the items on sale. They should use small amounts such as 2p or 4p so that the prices can be used in maths work.
● Read part 1 of the story on photocopiable page 33. At the point where reference is made to the shopping list, display an enlarged version of the list.
● Ask the children to help you read the words, focusing on sound-letter correspondences for example **br**ead, **ch**eese, **sh**ampoo and the length of words.
● Ask the children if they have written shopping lists or helped mum and dad write them. Ask if they write down things as they think of them or put them in the order they will collect them in the supermarket. For example, *What comes first in the supermarket?* (Usually fresh fruit and vegetables.) *Then what next? What areas do you go to for special things?* Consider areas such as take-away food, bakery, fish counter.
● Link the children's comments to their classroom supermarket in terms of its layout and the labels used. Collect any suggestions for further labels or special areas.

Shared word-level work

● Promote strategies for spelling by referring to the shopping list. Ask: *What do you do when you want to spell a new word?* Point to the words *tea bags*, for example, and ask the children how they knew what they say. They may say they have seen the words before and remember them, sounded them out or used initial letters then guessed.
● Go through several words on the list, writing the strategies on the board to provide a reminder throughout the unit.

Guided work

● Provide a selection of words associated with the topic for the children to read and practise using the spelling strategy 'Look, say, cover, write, check'.
● Encourage the children to draw upon the spelling strategies explored in whole-class work.

Independent work

● Organise the children to work in pairs to discuss photocopiable page 35. Tell them to apply the spelling strategies they discussed earlier in order to read the words from the jumbled list and put them in the right department of the supermarket.

Plenary

● Choose children who have completed photocopiable page 35 to explain the strategies they used to read new words and how they made their choices when organising items into departments.

UNIT 3 HOUR 3 ▪ Non-fiction 1

Using the supermarket 2

Objectives

NLS

T16: To write and draw simple instructions for everyday classroom use, e.g. in role-play area.
W10: To recognise the critical features of words, e.g. common spelling patterns and words within words.
W14: To form lower case letters correctly in a script that will be easy to join later.
S4: To write simple sentences and to re-read, recognising whether or not they make sense.

S&L

4 Drama: To explore familiar themes and characters through improvisation and role-play.

What you need
● Sugar-paper zigzag books
● plain white paper.

Differentiation

Less able
● Invite the children to use the supermarket for role-play. Ask the classroom assistant to support the children in discussing roles and responsibilities.
● After ten minutes children should draw a picture and write a simple instruction of what to do in one of the roles.

More able
● Ask pairs of children to write and draw instructions on how to use the supermarket, in response to one of the questions.

Shared text- and word-level work
● Before the session arrange for two pairs of children who have used the supermarket to explain to the other children how to use it.
● Use the children's input to develop the idea of writing simple instructions to remind everyone what to do.
● Display and read the following questions to elicit instructions from the children:

> ● What does the checkout person do?
> ● What do the shelf-stackers do?
> ● What do the customers do?

● Focus on one of the questions and write responses from the children. The response to question 1 might be, for example:

> ● The checkout person scans the goods.
> ● The checkout person takes the customers' money.
> ● The checkout person gives the customers their change.

● Use the term *sentence* when writing the children's responses pointing out how each sentence contains an action.
● Take the opportunity to demonstrate how to apply phonic and graphic knowledge for spelling and to reinforce correct letter formation.
● Tell the children that when writing their own instructions they may wish to depict what to do in a drawing.
● Recall the importance of lists and instructions, for example to help us remember what to buy, to help arrange things in the supermarket, as a reminder for spelling and to remind us what to do when using the supermarket role-play area.

Guided work
● Work with two groups of children to address one of the questions from shared work and demonstrate writing a set of instructions in the correct order.

Independent work
● Provide the children with colourful sugar-paper zigzag books in which to write and draw simple instructions for using the supermarket. They should write and draw on plain paper, which can then be stuck in the correct order in the book. The book will form their personal reminder of what to do when role-playing.

Plenary
● Display the instructions from the more able group and ask the other children to work with their partners to see if they have the same instructions. After a few minutes' discussion, choose one or two children to comment on the similarities and differences.

Internet shopping

Objectives

NLS
T12: To read and use captions, e.g. labels.
W8: To read on sight other familiar words, e.g. equipment labels, classroom captions.
W10: To recognise the critical features of words.

What you need

● Photocopiable pages 33, 34 and 35
● access to computers or an interactive whiteboard
● shopping baskets
● boxes for packing goods from the role-play area.

Shared text-level work

● Before the session prepare a spreadsheet similar to the order form on photocopiable page 36.
● Set up a laptop with projector or an interactive whiteboard. The aim of this activity is to give the children an experience of 'real-life' internet shopping.
● Begin the session by reading the second part of the shopping story on photocopiable page 34.
● Display the order form to demonstrate how Grandma, Beth and Mum used the computer to order goods.
● Demonstrate how to order goods by placing a number in the quantity column on the form.
● Involve the children in selecting goods and ordering them on the computer. You could use a numeracy lesson to work out the total order cost.

Shared word-level work

● Change the focus and concentrate on reading the words on the order form to reinforce different strategies for recognising less familiar words.
● The children should be able to recognise some words on sight from using them in the supermarket context. Encourage them to pick out words that they recognise.
● Then turn off the computer and involve the children in spelling, for example, *tin of beans* on the board. Ask one child to write *tin*, another to write *of* and finally another child to write *beans*.
● At each stage, ask the child to explain what strategies they are using to help them spell.
● Ask another child to check if the strategies used are on the class list, in order to encourage other children to refer to it.

Guided work

● Work with two groups of children using the whole story for guided reading. Reinforce strategies for reading new words.

Independent work

● Organise the children to work in pairs on computers to practise reading down the order form, selecting and ordering items.
● Tell them to put their names on their orders so that the supermarket will know who to deliver the order to.

Differentiation

Less able

● Ask the children to practise the process of placing an online order and discuss what will have to happen in the supermarket for the correct goods to be delivered.

More able

● Children could be given completed internet orders in order to gather the items in baskets, check them off on the printout and pack them in a box ready for delivery.

Plenary

● Discuss how to attend to online orders at the supermarket.
● Choose children who have used the supermarket to verify what happens.
● Explain to the children that they have now practised two ways of using a supermarket for their shopping – firstly they visited th to buy goods and then they ordered their shopping onlin

Making a timetable

Objectives

NLS
T15: To make simple lists for planning.
W8: To read on sight other familiar words, e.g. children's names.
W14: To form lower case letters correctly.

S&L
3 Group discussion and interaction: To ask and answer questions, make relevant contributions, offer suggestions and take turns.

What you need

● Photocopiable pages 37 (enlarged and, if possible, laminated) and 38
● goods, baskets and boxes in the role-play area
● Strips of card approximately 8cm x 3cm.

Shared text-level work

● Tell the children that now the supermarket is fully established, you want to make sure everyone has the chance to use it.
● Display the timetable on photocopiable page 37 and choose children to read the names of the days of the week.
● Explain that each day four groups can use the supermarket, one group before morning play, one after and so on. Read the first column.
● Show the children that by placing the groups' names in the boxes they can see when it is their turn to use the supermarket.

Shared word-level work

● Draw attention to the need for children to recognise each other's names, for the timetable and to deliver the online orders (see page 31).
● Write a child's name on the board, using a capital letter at the beginning, and carefully demonstrating the formation of the lower-case letters. Ask the children if they recognise the name. Do this again for another name.
● Ask the children to write their own names on their mini whiteboards. Observe the children and ask them to hold up their boards. Pick out one or two who are correctly forming difficult letters such as *p*, *d* and *b*, to demonstrate to others on the class board.

Guided work

● Support the more able group in writing lists of children's names so that the timetable can be completed.
● Reinforce using a capital letter at the beginning of a name and correct lower-case letter formation.
● Encourage the children to make relevant contributions and suggestions in devising the timetable.

Independent work

● Organise two groups to use the supermarket for approximately ten minutes each. During this time they should be responsible for making up the internet orders from yesterday and delivering them to the appropriate children.
● The other groups should complete photocopiable 38. As they copy the words, ask them to concentrate on correct letter formation.
● Also provide cards for children to write additional labels for the supermarket using words from the sheet.

Differentiation

Less able
● Provide support to ensure children write letters correctly when completing photocopiable page 38. Remind them to match word and picture first.

More able
● Give pairs of children the job of writing out each group's names on a card so that it can be attached to the timetable.

Plenary

● Choose two children from each group who organised the internet deliveries to describe what had to be done and how they organised who did what. Were there any problems and, if so, how did they overcome them?
● Display and read the timetable for next week.

A shopping list (1)

It was raining. Beth was stuck indoors. She played school with her dolls and teddy. Then she played tea parties. Then she dressed her toys for bed and tucked them up in her baby cot. Then – well then she was bored.

"What can I do now Mummy?" she called.

"Why don't you play school?" Mum replied.

"I've already played that." said Beth.

"What about tea parties?" suggested Mum.

"I've played that too."

Mum popped her head round the door and looked at Beth sympathetically. "I know what we'll do. We'll go shopping. You can help me to write the shopping list."

Beth's eyes lit up. She went quickly to the kitchen drawer and took out a notebook and pen, ready to write the shopping list.

"What do you think we need Beth?" Mum asked.

"We need some tea bags," said Beth. "Look, there aren't many in the jar."

"You're right," agreed Mum.

"And we need some washing-up liquid too; it's running out."

"So it is," said Mum.

"We need a pack of little apples for my packed lunch and cheese for my sandwiches. And bread. We always need bread."

"Would you write the list for me while I vacuum the living room?" Mum asked Beth. "Then we'll go to the supermarket."

So Beth wrote her list. It looked like this:

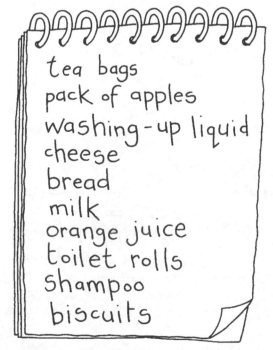

tea bags
pack of apples
washing-up liquid
cheese
bread
milk
orange juice
toilet rolls
shampoo
biscuits

Beth and Mum set off in the car to the supermarket. Inside, Beth used the list to help Mum collect all the shopping. She even ticked off the items on her list as they put them in the trolley.

It was still raining when they arrived home. "I'll help unpack too," said Beth.

"You're a real help," smiled Mum. "Maybe you could write the list next time we go shopping."

TERM 1

A shopping list (2)

The next day Grandma came for lunch. "I thought it would never stop raining yesterday; I couldn't go out at all," she said to Beth.

"We went shopping and I wrote the shopping list." replied Beth proudly.

"Well done!" said Grandma. "I wrote a shopping list too, but I didn't go out shopping," continued Grandma with a mischievous grin.

"Did the rain stop you going out?" asked Beth.

"Yes it did," said Grandma. "But it didn't stop me shopping." Grandma's grin broadened.

"What do you mean, Grandma?" asked Beth.

"Writing a shopping list is all I needed to do for my shopping."

Grandma paused but Beth was still puzzled, so Grandma explained: "I use the supermarket's internet shopping service. I choose items I want to buy on the computer and later in the day or the next day all my shopping is delivered to my home."

Beth thought it was a really good idea. "Can we do that Mum?" she asked. "Yes we can if you like, Beth. Maybe Grandma will show you how to do it."

So next time Beth's mum wanted some shopping she and Beth ordered it online.

Beth thought it was really exciting when the van delivered the shopping and she was eager to unpack the goods.

"Just a minute," said Mum. "We need to check that everything we asked for has been delivered. Call out the items as you take them out of the box and I'll tick them off on the printout."

Beth started unpacking. "Beans."

"Tinned or fresh?" asked Mum.

"Tinned," Beth continued. "Packet of ham, tin of soup."

"We ordered four tins of soup." said Mum.

"Oh yes, here they are: two tomato, two mushroom..."

Calling out the items and checking them against the list was harder than Beth had thought. It took a long time.

"There. Finished!" Mum said finally. "Now all we have to do is to put everything away. It seems to have taken as long as going to the supermarket ourselves!"

Supermarket sort

◼ Sort these items into the correct department.

fresh fish	vegetables	salad	bakery
delicatessen	take away	household	fruit

tomatoes	bread	cod	potatoes
	oranges	pizza	toilet rolls
pineapple	cakes	lettuce	bin liners
	carrots	tikka masala	ham

TERM 1

Online order form

Department	Item	Price each	Quantity (to be filled in by customer)	Cost of items
Bakery	Bread	4p		
	Cake	5p		
	Scone	2p		
	Bun	2p		
Fruit	Orange	3p		
	Apple	2p		
	Pear	2p		
	Pineapple	5p		
Vegetables	Potato	3p		
	Carrot	2p		
	Cauliflower	5p		
	Broccoli	4p		
			Total cost:	

Teacher's note: If this table is reproduced using Excel, you can introduce the standard formula to multiply the children's quantities by the item price to give the total cost per item. The item lines can then be summated to give the total list cost. Alternatively, children could calculate the totals themselves in a numeracy lesson.

Shopping timetable

	Monday	Tuesday	Wednesday	Thursday	Friday
Before morning play					
After morning play					
Before afternoon play					
After afternoon play					

TERM 1

Find the label

◼ Match the pictures and labels.

tomatoes	fish	ham	peas
apples	potatoes	meat	lettuce
cheese	beans	bread	biscuits

◣SCHOLASTIC

UNIT 4

Narrative 2

Using the traditional tale 'Chicken Licken', this unit comprises ten days' activities focusing on stories with predictable and repetitive patterns. The unit will help the children to develop an awareness of story structure and provide a real purpose for speaking and listening in talk partnerships. The focus of the first four sessions will be reading, leading to writing and constructing mini books in the following sessions. The activities in Hours 3 and 5 can be used in conjunction with *Progression in Phonics* Step 5, and Hours 7 and 9 with *Developing Early Writing* 'Developing the concept of a sentence'.

Hour	Shared text-level work	Shared word-/ sentence-level work	Guided work	Independent work	Plenary
1 First tellings	Listening to the story.	Reading high-frequency words.	Reading together, using a variety of reading strategies.	Playing a game with high-frequency word cards; adopting roles.	Re-enacting the story with props.
2 Re-enacting the story	Retelling the story with props.	Reading high-frequency words.	Reading together, using a variety of reading strategies.	Retelling the story using sentences and names on card to help; adopting roles.	Reading sentences from the story.
3 Oral and written stories	Comparing oral tale with written text.	Segmenting words by phonemes.	Practising letter formation.	Making words from phonemes.	Reading selected phonemes; using them in a sentence.
4 Story frieze	Telling the story by creating a wall frieze.	Revising phoneme knowledge and high-frequency words.	Reading the wall frieze.	Retelling the story in pictures.	Reading the wall frieze with expression.
5 Expanding the story	Composing additional sentences for the story frieze.	Segmenting phonemes.	Writing sentences to add to the story.	Add captions to their pictures.	Discussing differences between told and written stories.

UNIT 4

Hour	Shared text-level work	Shared word-/ sentence-level work	Guided work	Independent work	Plenary
6 Story books	Revising book features; suggesting a new title.	Using a writing frame to write story sentences.	Beginning to write own story books.	Using a writing frame to write own stories.	Discussing cover features.
7 The sentence	Writing story sentences.	Demarcating and identifying sentences.	Continuing to write own story books.	Continuing to write own story books.	Sharing and discussing the developing stories.
8 Improvising the story	Reading one of the children's stories to practise recall of events and characters; improvising events.	Noting key vocabulary and spelling patterns.	Continuing to write own story books.	Continuing to write own story books.; adding new words to class list.	Talking about new spellings.
9 Rehearsing the ending	Reading one version of a story and suggesting endings.	Writing a sentence to end the story.	Making book covers.	Continuing the story after discussion with talk partners.	Reading each other's stories; checking sense, spelling and punctuation.
10 Sharing stories	Revising cover features.	Pointing to words read and said; recognising names of classmates.	Making book covers.	Making book covers.	Reading stories to younger children and parents.

Key assessment opportunities

● Can the children talk about the differences between written and spoken forms?

● Did they read and/or re-enact stories with expression and intonation?

● Do they recognise high-frequency words?

● Can they use capital letters and full stops appropriately?

● Do they respond to what others say?

UNIT 4 HOUR 1 📄 Narrative 2

First tellings

Objectives

NLS

T7: To re-enact stories in a variety of ways, e.g. through role-play, using dolls or puppets.

W9: To read on sight approximately 30 high-frequency words from Appendix List 1.

S&L

4 Drama: to explore familiar themes and characters through improvisation and role play.

What you need

● Photocopiable pages 51 and 52
● an enlarged version of the first bubble on photocopiable page 53
● the word *we* on card at a size that it can replace *I* in the text
● characters and names from photocopiable pages 54 and 55 attached to lollipop sticks
● sets of high-frequency word cards in cloth bags
● a simple glove puppet of Chicken Licken
● a farmyard setting as part of role-play area
● character masks made from paper plates attached to dowels.

Differentiation

Less able

● Choose a group to use the farmyard role-play area to act out the story. Let them use the masks to help them take on roles. Reassure them that they do not have to be accurate in their re-enacting as oral stories are different.

More able

● Ask the children to work in pairs to tell the story to each other using the speech bubbles and characters' names.

Shared text-level work

● Before the lesson, familiarise yourself with the story from photocopiable pages 51 and 52. Embellish the story differently each time you tell it, perhaps asking the children to choose new characters for Chicken Licken to meet.
● Tell the story, including suitable dramatic effect.
● Tell the story again, but this time display the sentence *The sky is falling down and I am going to tell the King* and refer to the words as you say them. Involve the children in reading by:

> ● using a pointer to point to the words as they are spoken
> ● changing I to we as necessary, emphasising the different look of the words and the letters used
> ● using pictures and names of the characters; choose children to match the picture of the character to the name and hold them up for others to see.

Shared word-level work

● Hold up some of the high-frequency word cards and ask the children if they can spot any of these words in the displayed sentence from the story.
● Mix up the cards in a bag and select different children to put on the glove puppet of Chicken Licken in order to pick a card from the bag and say the word aloud. Ask if they can see it in the sentence.

Guided work

● As the children take turns to read the story, concentrate on reading strategies.
● Help the children to recognise the look of high-frequency words (as practised in shared work) and use the grammar of the sentence to predict meaning. Also encourage them to determine characters' names from initial sounds and to blend sounds together (covered further on pages 43, 44 and 45). Suggest other reading strategies, for example analogy or words within words.

Independent work

● Organise the children to work in groups of two or three, each with a cloth bag of selected high-frequency words (including those from shared work). Ask them to play a game of picking out words and reading them aloud to each other.
● Allow groups to take turns with the Chicken Licken puppet as part of the game.

Plenary

● Choose two children from the role-play group (see Differentiation) to show the others how they have used the masks to re-enact the story. Ask one of the children to be Chicken Licken, the other to be Turkey Lurkey and act out the repetitive line in the story: *The sky is falling down and I am going to tell the King.*

UNIT 4 HOUR 2 Narrative 2

Re-enacting the story

Objectives

NLS

T7: To re-enact stories in a variety of ways, e.g. through role-play, using dolls or puppets.
W9: To read on sight approximately 30 high-frequency words from Appendix List 1.

What you need

- Photocopiable pages 51 and 52
- enlarged speech bubbles from photocopiable page 53
- masks of the characters
- envelopes containing sets of the characters' names and speech bubbles from photocopiable pages 53 and 54 attached to lollipop sticks
- a simple glove puppet of Chicken Licken
- cloth bags of high-frequency word cards
- the farmyard role-play area

Differentiation

Less able
- Provide support so that children who need help recognising high-frequency words can play the game.

More able
- Ask children to re-enact the story in the role-play area with the correct sequence of events.

Shared text-level work

- Tell the children that you are going to ask for their help in retelling the story of Chicken Licken.
- Remind them that when we tell stories they do not need to be exactly the same as the written version and that the storyteller can use his or her own style.
- Ask what Chicken Licken says when she meets the other animals. (*The sky is falling down and I am going to tell the King.*)
- Display the enlarged sentence and pick a child to read aloud as he or she points to the words.
- Display the response *Then I shall come too* and again pick a child to point and read.
- Choose eight children to play the story characters with the appropriate masks. (The characters are Chicken Licken, Henny Penny, Cocky Locky, Ducky Lucky, Drakey Lakey, Goosey Loosey, Turkey Lurkey and Foxy Loxy.)
- Retell the story, embellishing it as you go along, with the children using the masks contributing, from memory, the words spoken by their characters.
- Point to the sentences as they are spoken.

Shared word-level work

- Introduce the Chicken Licken glove puppet and say that she wants to play the game of picking a word from the cloth bag and reading it out aloud.
- Explain that Chicken Licken often gets things wrong and may need some help.
- Then proceed to use the puppet to pick a word from the bag. Say the wrong word and ask the children to help her say the right word.
- Use this as an opportunity to assess which children can recognise high-frequency words.

Guided work

- Continue as Hour 1, working with a different group of children and concentrating on reading strategies.

Independent work

- Organise the children to work in pairs.
- Provide each pair with an envelope containing the characters' names and speech bubbles.
- Ask the pairs to tell the story to each other using the cards.

Plenary

- Display the speech bubbles from photocopiable page 53. Choose children to point to and read the sentences aloud. Repeat this with different sentences.
- To reinforce reading strategies, ask the children what they can do if they can't read a word.

Oral and written stories

Objectives

NLS
T3: To notice the difference between spoken and written forms through retelling known stories; compare oral versions with the written text.
W14: To form lower case letters correctly in a script that will be easy to join later.

What you need

● Photocopiable pages 51 and 52
● a Big Book version of 'Chicken Licken' (see Shared text-level work)
● a glove puppet of Chicken Licken
● a cloth bag of word cards from photocopiable page 56 and sets for group work
● phoneme cards from photocopiable page 56 in envelopes.

Differentiation

Less able

● Give the children the words from photocopiable page 56 and work with them to practise segmenting them by phonemes. Segment the words by cutting them into phonemes or marking the breaks with pen.

More able

● Ask the children to segment the words from photocopiable page 56 by marking the phonemes with a pen.

Shared text-level work

● Before the session make a Big Book. Join two A2 cards lengthways with wide tape to make a hinged spine, then make further leaves by joining them in the same way. Enlarge appropriate sections from photocopiable pages 51 and 52 and paste them into the book. Leave pages (or spaces on pages) for children's illustrations.
● This session explores the differences between spoken and written texts by comparing oral versions of 'Chicken Licken' with the written form. (These differences are not easy to convey to young children. This activity gives a general idea of some key language differences, which is all that is required at this level.)
● Display your Big Book of 'Chicken Licken'.
● Follow the text and read the story to the children.
● Ask the children what differences they notice between telling the story in earlier sessions and reading the story today. The children should point out that the told story changed each time, that some descriptions were added, that sometimes there was no need to say who was speaking or how they were speaking.
● Some further questions to ask are: *What were the changes in the told story? Could you tell how Chicken Licken was feeling by the way she sounded? Was there anything in the text to help you know?*

Shared word-level work

● Wear the glove puppet of Chicken Licken. Explain that just as she needed help with her words, she also needs help to understand individual sounds so the children have to talk to her in phonemes.
● Take one word card from the cloth bag and ask the children what it is. Ask them to tell Chicken Licken what it is, by sounding out the phonemes, for example *ch/i/ck, d/u/ck*. To ensure all children are involved, ask them to say the phonemes to their partner first, then choose different children to say them to Chicken Licken.
● Reinforce the *ck* consonant digraph by demonstrating how to write the letters correctly.

Guided work

● Choose children to demonstrate the formation of their letters as in shared work and then follow this as a group in handwriting practice.

Independent work

● Organise the children into pairs and provide each pair with an envelope of phonemes. Challenge the children to use the phonemes to create words.

Plenary

● Choose children who have been making words from phonemes to show and read a selection of the words they have made.
● Challenge the children to make up a sentence using a word a child has made.

Story frieze

Objectives

NLS
T3: To notice the differences between spoken and written forms through retelling known stories.
T4: To point while reading and make correspondence between words said and read.
S3: To read with appropriate expression and intonation, e.g. in reading to others.

What you need

● A wall prepared with frieze paper to use as a storyboard
● speech bubbles, labels and illustrations from photocopiable pages 53-55
● photocopiable page 57, cut into strips
● A3 paper
● painting materials
● an envelope containing speech bubbles from photocopiable page 53 and characters from page 54 to match sentences on photocopiable page 57.

Differentiation

Less able
● Invite the children to paint the characters that have been stuck on to the frieze (remove them first!), then ask them to replace the figures on the frieze in the right order, to consolidate their understanding of the sequence of events.

More able
● Give pairs of children sentence numbers 6 to 9 from the sheet to work with.

Shared text-level work

● Gather the children in front of the wall that you have prepared with frieze paper. Explain that you are going to choose some of them to retell the story by using the wall like a storyboard. Tell them that they are going to use speech bubbles and pictures of the characters to stick on to the frieze as the story is being told. The wall frieze can then be used to help others tell the story.
● Remind the children that speech bubbles contain the words that characters say to each other.
● Help the children to retell the story. Read and select appropriate speech bubbles and choose character pictures to stick in sequence on the wall frieze. Provide opportunities for children to point while reading the speech bubbles, making links between words said and read.
● If children have come up with new characters, ask them to draw the new figures and add labels from photocopiable page 54.

Shared word-level work

● Integrate word-level work into the shared text-level session by asking children to identify and read high-frequency words in the speech bubbles as you go along.
● Also emphasise the phonemes in the words *Chicken* and *Ducky*. Encourage the children to apply their knowledge from the previous day's work to segment the words by phonemes: *Ch/i/ck/e/n, D/u/ck/y*.

Guided work

● Help one or two groups to read the story from the wall frieze in preparation for reading it to the class in plenary.

Independent work

● Organise the children in pairs or groups of three. Give the children one of the first five statements from photocopiable page 57, A3 paper and art materials, and the appropriate envelope of characters and speech bubbles.
● Tell the children to work together to paint the scene from the story described in the sentence they have been given. Tell them to place the characters' speech bubbles and sentence appropriately on their sheet of paper and to draw a background scene. The background could be a farmyard or a wood where the acorn falls on Chicken Licken's head.
● These pictures should then be displayed under the wall frieze in the correct story sequence to reinforce and enhance the story. (Embellish the wall frieze further by linking this topic to art where an appropriate painted background could be painted using the ideas from these paintings).

Plenary

● Choose two children at a time to read the speech bubbles in a particular section of the wall frieze. Encourage them to read with expression.

Expanding the story

Objectives

NLS

T8: Through shared and guided writing to apply phonological, graphic knowledge and sight vocabulary to spell CVC words accurately.

W4: To discriminate and segment all three phonemes in words.

What you need

● The wall frieze created in Hour 4.

Shared text-level work

● The children should now be familiar with the story, so choose volunteers to use the wall frieze to retell the story.

● Ask the children to point to the dialogue as they tell the story, to reinforce the link between spoken words and written text.

● Ask the children if they could add anything to the story. For example, would it be useful/interesting to write more about how the story begins and ends?

● Work with the children to compose a beginning and an ending for the story using their own words.

● Model the beginning and ending first on the board. Articulate the writer's thought processes and discuss the choices that need to be made as you write – for example what words to use and how to order them.

● Continue to scribe for the children, involving them fully in the choices being made.

● Add this writing to the frieze, perhaps editing for a last time as you write.

Shared word-level work

● Reinforce phonic work about segmenting.

● Tell the children you want to write the word *p/a/ck*. Write the first two letters on the board in a three-phoneme frame (*p/a/*).

● Ask the children what sound is at the end of the word. Then ask them what the sound looks like.

● Choose a child to write the sound on the board. (You can check that the child is forming letters correctly as well as knowing the spelling for the sound.)

● Do this with a few more three-phoneme words ending in *ck* for example *sack* and *peck*.

Guided work

● Ask the children to add to the wall frieze story. They could add extra detail to the middle part of the story. For example, they could write sentences to describe what each character was doing just before she or he met Chicken Licken.

Differentiation

Less able

● Ask the children to write a sentence about the character they painted for the frieze.

More able

● Ask the children to discuss and write a different ending to the story. Ensure their contributions are included in the plenary.

Independent work

● Organise the children who made a picture of a scene from the story back into their pairs or groups of three.

● Challenge them to caption their scene by writing sentences for their part of the story.

Plenary

● Choose some of the children's writing to further explain the difference between told stories and written versions. If possible, choose children from each group.

● Encourage more able children to share their endings.

UNIT 4 HOUR 6 Narrative 2

Storybooks

Objectives

NLS
T9: To write about events in personal experience linked to a variety of familiar incidents from stories.
T11: To make simple picture storybooks with sentences, modelling them on basic text conventions, e.g. cover, title, layout.
S4: To write simple sentences, and to re-read, recognising whether or not they make sense.

What you need
● The class Big Book from Hour 3
● a Big Book of another traditional tale
● photocopiable pages 58 and 59.

Differentiation

Less able
● Provide sets of word cards to support children in forming ideas.
● Tell them to write their ideas on the photocopiable sheets, then cut these out each day to add to their own book as it develops.

More able
● Help children to create a book cover for the class Big Book including illustrations and a title they decide on.

Shared text-level work
● Tell the children that it would be a good idea to use their Big Book of 'Chicken Licken' to read to children in Reception. Explain that the book needs to be just like a 'bought' book.
● Make a comparison between the class Big Book and a commercial Big Book. Pick out conventions such as cover, title, author and layout of pictures and text.
● Ask questions about the cover of the commercial book for children to see how the cover offers clues about the story. Then ask them what should be included on a cover for 'Chicken Licken'. Collect the ideas on the board.
● Consider a title for this 'Chicken Licken' story and collect these on the board. It will be difficult to make a direct comparison regarding the author's name so explain that some stories are so old that nobody can remember who first told them.

Shared sentence-level work
● Tell the children that they are going to make a little story book of their own. Say that this will be read to younger children as well as to each other.
● Begin by making a direct comparison to the opening of 'Chicken Licken', saying that we often set out to tell someone about something special that has happened to us and that this event will form the basis of their story. For example: *My wobbly tooth has fallen out, I lost my shoe, I found 20p, My dog ran off.*
● Display photocopiable pages 58 and 59, read them together and make the point of rehearsing ideas on notepaper. Fill in the sentence spaces for page 1 with the children's suggestions, letting them choose from the word bank on the sheet.

Guided work
● Work with a different group of children each day over the next five days to support their writing for their own storybooks.
● Scribe and support the composition as appropriate, making reference to the model on the photocopiable sheet.

Independent work
● Provide the children with note paper on which to rehearse ideas and A4 paper folded in half to create four pages.
● Ask the children to begin their own story using photocopiable page 58. Encourage them to use their own ideas and try to spell words using conventions such as 'Look, say, cover, write, check'.
● Store the children's work safely in plastic wallets in a ring binder.

Plenary
● Ask the more able group (see Differentiation) to present their work and to explain how the drawings provide clues about the story and how they chose the title.

The sentence

Shared text-level work
● Display an enlarged copy of a child's sentence from Hour 6.
● Involve the children in reading the sentence and pointing to words as they are read.
● Use the class Big Book to remind the children what happens in the story after this sentence and how we can use the text from the story to help continue our own story.
● Display photocopiable page 58 and help the children to compose their own sentence for page 2. You will need to point out the reason for changing Chicken Licken to I.
● Construct this sentence: *So I set off to tell ___ ___, but before very long I met ___ ___.*
● Ask questions that encourage the children to think of a developing story, for example: *Who would you want to tell and why would you choose them? Who might you meet? Why would you want to meet them? What would you tell them?*
● Remind the children of the purpose of their composition: to write their own stories to read to younger children and each other.
● Encourage the children to provide extra information about who they want to tell or who they meet, for example *my brother Darren, Mr Goldsworthy, my friend Sasha.*

Shared sentence-level work
● Using the sentence that you have composed with the children, point out the capital letter to start the sentence and the full stop to end it.
● Refer to yesterday's sentence (page 1) and ask a child to point to the beginning to check if it begins with a capital letter. Ask another child to point to the end and add a full stop if necessary.
● Ask volunteers to explain how to begin and end a sentence.

Guided work
● Continue as Hour 6, using the sentence for page 2 of the story book model on photocopiable page 58.

Independent work
● Provide model sentences 1 and/or 2 appropriate to the needs of the child (some may be working faster than others) and ask the children to continue their stories. You may also wish to provide notepaper so that the children can trial ideas and spellings.
● Encourage the children to refer to their first sentence so that they can construct a sentence that says what happens next.

Plenary
● Ask the children to share and discuss their work with a partner at their table.
● Encourage the children to read each other's stories. Then choose children to talk about their partner's story to the class. Discuss some of the interesting ideas that come up.

Improvising the story

Objectives

NLS

T5: To describe story settings and incidents and relate them to own experience and that of others.

W12: To learn new words from reading and shared experiences, and to make collections of personal interest or significant words.

S&L

4 Drama: To explore familiar themes through improvisation.

What you need

● Enlarged version of a child's story so far
● a large sheet entitled 'New words' fixed to the wall
● photocopiable page 59
● A2 coloured card.

Differentiation

Less able

● Help the children to concentrate on using the sentence starters for page 3.

More able

● Provide the children with A2 coloured card on which to try out spellings for new words, for sharing in the plenary.

Shared text-level work

● Read what has happened so far in one child's story. (Make sure the child is aware this is going to happen and is praised for his or her work.)
● Tell the children that they are going to act out their own story in their heads. Tell them to imagine themselves walking or cycling in the park or in the wood or wherever their story starts, until you say 'Stop'.
● Then ask them to turn to the person next to them and tell each other what has happened and who they are on their way to tell. Allow appropriate time and ask classroom assistants to encourage dialogue between the children.
● At an appropriate point stop the children and ask them to discuss with their talk partner what might happen next in their story, who else they might meet and what they will tell them.
● Next time you stop, tell the children to remember their story so that they are ready to continue writing.

Shared word-level work

● Point out the special words the child has used for describing the day, setting and what happened, for example *rainy, park, cycling.* Ask the children to think about what is going to happen next in their story and what words to use.
● Choose a child to tell you what is going to happen next and, with the other children, choose an interesting word from what is said in order to explore the spelling. Ask questions such as: *What letter does it start with? What sounds can you hear next? Do you know the spelling pattern? Have you seen it some where before? What sound can you hear at the end?*
● Do this again for another word in order to develop phonological awareness or links with analogous spelling patterns.
● Add these words to 'New words' and encourage children to add to it as they write.

Guided work

● Continue as Hour 6, using page 3 of the story book model on photocopiable page 59.

Independent work

● Tell the children that they are going to continue their story using the skills they practised in shared work. They should use a sentence starter from page 3 to help them write who they meet next.
● Ask the children to add new words to the sheet for others to see.

Plenary

● Ask the more able group to talk about how they attempted to spell new words. Allow the rest of the children to contribute so that correct spellings are arrived at.
● Look at the sounds of words on the wall sheet and check for correct spellings.

Rehearse the ending

Objectives

NLS

T9: To write about events in personal experience, linked to a variety of familiar incidents from stories.

S4: To write simple sentences, and to re-read, recognising whether or not they make sense.

S9: To use a capital letter for the personal pronoun *I* and for the start of a sentence.

S&L

1 Speaking: To describe incidents or tell stories from their own experience, in an audible voice.

What you need

● Enlarged version of a child's story so far
● Photocopiable page 59.

Shared text-level work

● Organise the children so that they are sitting in their talk partnerships from Hour 8. Make sure the child whose story you have chosen is happy to proceed.

● Read the story so far with the children and ask for suggestions about what might happen next. Ask the child whose story is being displayed what he or she had planned to happen, and if his or her talk partner agrees.

● Now tell the children that they are to discuss between talk partners how this particular story might end.

● After an appropriate time, stop the children and choose two or three pairs to share their ideas. Ensure that the child who wrote the story has a chance to offer his or her pair's ideas.

Shared sentence-level work

● Use the child's suggested ending and model writing it on the board, using page 4 from photocopiable page 59. Rehearse the sentence orally before writing.

● Begin with a lower case letter to see if the children spot your mistake.

● Encourage the children to assist you with spelling and involve them in reading and re-reading to check for coherence and flow.

● Talk about grammatical features, especially the full stop at the end of sentences and the capital letter for the personal pronoun I.

● Go over what you have done:

1. Practised saying the sentence that is the ending of the story.
2. Tried out spellings.
3. Read and re-read for sense.
4. Used a capital letter to start the sentence and a full stop to end.

Guided work

● Continue as for Hour 6, using page 4 of the story book model on photocopiable page 59.

Independent work

● Rearranged furniture often encourages children to focus on the task in hand, so arrange the furniture so that talk partners are a distinctive feature and have some privacy for discussion and collaboration.

● Ask the children to rehearse their story ending orally with their partner then write the ending of their story on the last page of their little book.

Plenary

● Combine the talk partners into groups of four to share their stories. Demonstrate how to take turns so that each child has the opportunity to read.

● Encourage the children to read each other's stories checking for sense, spelling, capital letters at the start of the sentence and full stops at the end.

Differentiation

Less able

● Let the children work closely with talk partners to complete page 4 on photocopiable page 59.

More able

● Give the children the additional challenge of trying out spellings and making collections of new words using cards from Hour 8.

UNIT 4 HOUR 10 ◻ Narrative 2

Sharing stories

Objectives

NLS
T11: To make simple picture storybooks, modelling them on basic text conventions, e.g. cover, author's name, title.
S5: To recognise full stops and capital letters when reading, and name them correctly.
W8: To read on sight other familiar words, e.g. children's names.

S&L
1 Speaking: To describe incidents or tell stories from their own experience, in an audible voice.

What you need
● The class Big Book from Hour 6
● a child's story that features names of other children in the class
● scrap paper
● coloured card covers for the children's stories
● cartridge paper slightly smaller than the card front cover.

Differentiation

Less able
● Scribe titles and demonstrate spelling strategies and correct letter formation.

More able
● Ask the children to try out various layouts which could include 'wrapping' text around their picture.

Shared text-level work
● Prior to this session arrange for a joint plenary/story session with Reception, perhaps in the hall, where the two classes can share the storybooks. You may also want to invite parents.
● Organise the children into their talk partnerships from Hour 8.
● Remind the children of the features of a book cover using the class Big Book.
● Draw attention to the layout of the title, telling the children that their covers will also need their name as author of the story.
● Read the Big Book story to the children. Ask questions such as:
- *What makes a good title?*
- *What picture could you put on the cover that would give clues about the story?*
- *How would you provide a clue about where he/she was going, and whom he/she was going to tell?*
- *Do we want to keep some things in the story secret?*
● Then ask the children to talk to their partners about their cover ideas for about five minutes.

Shared word- and sentence-level work
● Read the other story with the children, ensuring that the children can make correspondence between the word read and said by letting them use the pointer.
● Check if they can recognise on sight the names of classmates used in the story.
● Involve the children in talking about spellings and the use of punctuation.

Guided and independent work
● Explain to the children that they are going to make front covers for their stories.
● Ask them to work with their talk partners to decide on how to set out their titles and names on the front cover.
● Before writing, advise them to try out difficult spellings and different layouts on scrap paper and check their ideas with their partner.
● Also tell the children to draw a picture clue on the cover, again sketching on paper first.
● When the children are happy with the layouts for their front cover, the children can create final versions on cartridge paper.
● The cartridge paper can then be stuck on to the card covers and secured to the story pages.

Plenary
● Ensure that the covers are secured to the pages, then organise for an extended plenary of about 20 minutes where the children can read their stories to younger children and parents.
● Display the books on flat bookshelves so that they can be read during the forthcoming weeks.

The Story of Chicken Licken

One bright autumn morning Chicken Licken was walking in the wood when an acorn fell on her head with a great big BUMP.

"Oh no," she said. "I must tell the King that the sky is falling down."

So she set off to tell the King, but before very long she met her friend Henny Penny.

"Where are you going?" asked Henny Penny.

"The sky is falling down and I am going to tell the King," Chicken Licken replied.

"Then I shall come too."

So they cheeped and clucked as they went on their way to see the King.

Soon they met Cocky Locky. "Where are you two going in such a hurry?" he asked.

"The sky is falling down and we are going to tell the King."

"Then I will come too."

So they cheeped and clucked and crowed as they went on their way to see the King.

After a while they met Ducky Lucky. "Where are you all going in such a hurry?" she asked.

"The sky is falling down and we are going to tell the King."

"Then I will come too."

So they cheeped and clucked and crowed and quacked as they went on their way to see the King.

After a while they met Drakey Lakey. "Where are you all going in such a hurry?" he asked.

"The sky is falling down and we are going to tell the King."

"Then I will come too."

So they cheeped and clucked and crowed and quacked and cackled as they went on their way to see the King.

After a while they met Goosey Loosey. "Where are you all going in such a hurry?" he asked.

"The sky is falling down and we are going to tell the King."

"Then I will come too."

So they cheeped and clucked and crowed and quacked and cackled and honked as they went on their way to see the King.

Soon they met Turkey Lurkey. "Where are you all going in such a hurry?" he asked.

"The sky is falling down and we are going to tell the King."

"Then I will come too."

So they cheeped and clucked and crowed and quacked and cackled and honked and gobbled as they went on their way to see the King.

Then they met Foxy Loxy. "Where are you all going in such a hurry this bright autumn morning?" he asked cheerfully.

"We are going to tell the King that the sky is falling down."

"Oh dear," said Foxy Loxy. "Follow me, I know where to find the King."

So Chicken Licken, Henny Penny, Cocky Locky, Ducky Lucky, Drakey Lakey, Goosey Loosey and Turkey Lurkey followed Foxy Loxy, but instead of taking them to the King he led them into his den where he ate them all up.

Speech bubbles

The sky is falling down and I am going to tell the King.

Then I shall come too.

Follow me, I know where to find the King.

Where are you going in such a hurry?

TERM 1

Character name labels

Chicken Licken	Cocky Locky
Drakey Lakey	Turkey Lurkey
Henny Penny	Ducky Lucky
Goosey Loosey	Foxy Loxy

■SCHOLASTIC

Characters

Phoneme cards

a	e	i	o	u
b	c	ch	d	f
l	p	r	s	sh
ck	ck	ck	ck	ck

chick	pack	duck
sack	lick	block
frock	flock	shock
peck	sock	pick
cock	lock	luck

▪ SCHOLASTIC

The events of the story

1. Chicken Licken thinks the sky is falling down.

2. Chicken Licken tells Henny Penny.

3. Chicken Licken and Henny Penny tell Cocky Locky.

4. Chicken Licken, Henny Penny and Cocky Locky tell Ducky Lucky.

5. Chicken Licken, Henny Penny, Cocky Locky and Ducky Lucky tell Drakey Lakey.

6. Chicken Licken, Henny Penny, Cocky Locky, Ducky Lucky and Drakey Lakey tell Goosey Loosey.

7. Chicken Licken, Henny Penny, Cocky Locky, Ducky Lucky, Drakey Lakey and Goosey Loosey tell Turkey Lurkey.

8. Chicken Licken, Henny Penny, Cocky Locky, Ducky Lucky, Drakey Lakey, Goosey Loosey and Turkey Lurkey meet Foxy Loxy.

9. The fox tricks Chicken Licken, Henny Penny, Cocky Locky, Ducky Lucky, Drakey Lakey, Goosey Loosey and Turkey Lurkey and eats them all up.

Story book model (1)

Page 1

One day on a _____ I was _____

in the _____ when _____

snowy   windy   rainy   sunny

showery   foggy   freezing   warm

morning   afternoon

walking   cycling   running   skipping   playing

park   play ground   street   field

woods   shopping centre   supermarket

Page 2

So I set off to tell _____ but before

very long I met _____

the   my

friend   brother   sister   teacher

Story book model (2)

Page 3

After a while I met _____

Soon I met _____

or

Then I met _____

Page 4

So _____, _____, and I went _____

to tell _____ that _____

UNIT 5

Poetry 2

This five-hour unit uses two traditional nursery rhymes to address in particular the art of reciting, dramatisation of story and phonological awareness to support reading and writing. Reading aloud expressively is a major focus for this unit. Work in Hour 1 links to *Progression in Phonics* Step 4 and Hour 2 links to Step 5.

Hour	Shared text-level work	Shared word-/ sentence-level work	Guided work	Independent work	Plenary
1 Learning to recite	Reciting the rhyme and exploring new words.	Identifying and suggesting new words rhyming with the long vowel sound *o*.	Developing awareness of reading strategies.	Matching rhyming phrases to pictures.	Reciting the rhyme; practising long *o* sound spelling patterns.
2 Inventing rhymes	Inventing rhymes using 'Blow wind blow' as a model.	Segmenting initial, medial and final phonemes.	Beginning to write creatively using the structure of 'Blow wind blow'.	Beginning to write creatively using the structure of 'Blow wind blow' and their own names.	Reading aloud their own rhymes.
3 Dramatisation	Working through the rhyme, finding ways to act each 'scene'.		Continuing to write creatively using the structure of 'Blow wind blow'.	Reading their poems to classmates; generating further rhymes.	Discussing poems read aloud.
4 The north wind doth blow	Reading and reciting the rhyme.	Pointing to words said and read; generating rhymes.	Practising reading strategies for new and unfamiliar words.	Reassembling jumbled lines of the rhyme; reading with expression.	Presenting the drama.
5 Rhyming words 💬	Recalling and reciting the rhyme.	Generating lists of rhyming words.	Reading with expression and intonation.	Sorting words into rhyming sets; generating rhyming words.	Group and whole-class performance of the rhyme.

Key assessment opportunities

● Can the children recite rhymes with appropriate expression, tone, rhythm and volume?

● Can they think of rhyming words and recognise different spelling patterns?

● Can they use rhymes as a model for their own writing?

Learning to recite

Objectives
T4: To read poems independently, to point while reading and make correspondence between words said and read.
T6: To recite stories and rhymes with predictable and repeating patterns.
W10: To recognise the critical features of words, e.g. common spelling patterns.

What you need
● Photocopiable pages 66-68
● the text and pictures from photocopiable page 67, cut up and jumbled in envelopes (one for each child)
● A4 sugar paper.

Shared text-level work
● Recite 'Blow wind blow' with appropriate expression, intonation, pace and volume. (Don't display the rhyme at this point.)
● Ask the children what they think the rhyme is about, then ask what words from the rhyme helped them to know what it is about.
● Read the rhyme again and continue to ask questions to help the children describe the pictures the rhyme conjures in their minds.
● Display photocopiable page 67 and explain how the wind drives the sails that drive the millstones that grind the corn into flour.
● Display the rhyme and read it aloud together. Model reading expressively. Point to the words as they are read.

Shared word-level work
● Focus on words that rhyme with *blow* and *go*. Ask the children to identify the rhyming words in the poem and list these on the board.
● Emphasise that *blow* and *go* have the same rhyming sound even though the spelling patterns are different.
● On one side of the board write *blow* as a column heading, and on the other side *go*.
● As the children suggest words, for example *snow, mow, so, no*, list them under the appropriate spelling pattern. Establish the meanings of the words as you go.
● If the children suggest rhyming words with different spelling patterns, such as *sew, dough, hoe, toe, oh*, write these in between the two columns.
● Conclude by choosing children to read and say some of the words, drawing attention to the same sound but lots of different spelling patterns.

Guided work
● Use the rhyme for guided reading, encouraging the children to discuss the strategies they are using to read new words.
● Also provide time for the children to read the rhyme independently.

Independent work
● Give the children the envelopes containing the jumbled-up text and pictures from photocopiable page 67 and a sheet of sugar paper.
● Ask the children to read the text and look at the pictures carefully. When they have matched them correctly, they should stick down the pictures and words together in the correct order.

Plenary
● Ask the children who have been learning the rhyme (see Differentiation) to recite it for the class.
● Provide mini whiteboards for children to write spellings of 'o' words, such as *snow* and *blow*, as you say them. Choose volunteers to write them on the class board at the same time so that the children can decide on the correct spellings.

Differentiation

Less able
● Provide pairs with three sets of coloured counters, for example red, blue and yellow and photocopiable page 68. Ask the children to sort the spelling patterns by placing counters over the words, for example all yellow counters on *ow* words.

More able
● Ask the children to read and learn the rhyme in order to recite it as a group.

Inventing rhymes

Objectives
T10: To use rhymes as models for their own writing.
W1: To generate rhyming strings.
W10: To recognise the critical features of words, e.g. common spelling patterns.

What you need
● Photocopiable page 66.

Shared text-level work

● Ask the children if they can remember the rhyme from Hour 1. Choose a child to recite it and others to help if necessary.
● Suggest making up a new rhyme but instead of the words *wind* and *mill* use a child's name instead, for example *Blow Charlotte blow! And go Charlotte go!*
● Write on the board *That Charlotte may...* and ask the children to suggest what Charlotte might be blowing, for example *bubbles in the sky*, *balloons for her party*, *the whistle for playtime*.
● Ask the children what other words rhyming with *blow* could be used to make up rhymes about other children, for example *Snow Edward snow! No Edward no!*
● Playing with the rhyming words in this way should elicit much fun and provide opportunity for exploring rhyme.
● Continue to write children's suggested concluding sentences: *That Edward might build a snowman* and so on.

Shared word-level work

● Focus on words rhyming with *mill*. Ask the children to identify each sound in the word *mill*: *m, i, ll*.
● Then ask the children if they can think of other words that rhyme with *mill*.
● Some of the children's suggestions will be real words, such as *frill* and others may be nonsense words: *zill*; accept either, sounding out each grapheme as you write the word on the board.
● Draw attention to the medial *i* sound and suggest other end sounds, such as *i* and *t* as in *mit* and *sit*.
● Choose children to write words rhyming with a word you suggest, for example *pit, bin* and *dim*.

Guided work

● Use the structure of 'Blow wind blow' as a model for writing a new version as a group poem, building on the children's ideas from shared text-level work.
● Demonstrate rhymes and the construction of lines, and scribe where necessary in order that the children are supported in beginning to create original rhymes.

Independent work

● Working individually, ask the children to make up rhymes based on 'Blow wind blow', using their own name and words rhyming with *blow* and *go*.
● Explain to the children that they will be able to make additions to their rhymes in the next session.

Plenary

● Choose children to read out their rhymes. Encourage them to read with intonation, expression and volume.

Differentiation

Less able
● Provide a set of words, for example *mill, pin, sit* and *dim* for each pair. One child should choose a word to read and the other should write and read as many rhyming words as she or he can. The children should then swap roles.

More able
● Encourage the children to invent a concluding sentence to their rhyme.

Dramatisation

Objectives
T7: To re-enact stories in a variety of ways.
T10: To use rhymes as models for their own writing.
W1: To practise and secure the ability to rhyme through exploring rhyming patterns and generating rhyming strings.

What you need
● Photocopiable pages 66 and 68
● the children's rhymes from Hour 2
● a bag of rhyming word cards.

Shared text-level work
● Create a space large enough for drama work. Tell the children that they are going to act out the rhyme 'Blow wind blow'.
● Organise the children into groups of four, then act out the rhyme step by step:

> ● Blow wind blow!: Tell the children to be the wind, blowing as mightily as they can.
> ● And go mill go!: The children need to imagine themselves as the windmill sails turning round and round.
> ● That the miller may grind his corn: Choose a group to help you demonstrate the action of the miller pouring corn into the mill to be ground by the huge turning millstones. Each child could be given a part – the miller pouring, the millstones turning and grinding. Then tell the other groups to act out this part of the rhyme.
> ● That the baker may take it/And into bread make it: This time you want each group to think of their own way of acting this out. Observe the groups and after an appropriate time choose one to demonstrate to the rest of the class.
> ● And bring us some fresh in the morn: Ask the children what they think is happening, and how they might represent this in drama. Allow time for the groups to act out the line.

● Conclude the session by telling the children that some of them will put all their actions together to tell the whole rhyme through drama.

Guided work
● Work with two groups to support writing of additional rhyming phrases for their poems.

Independent work
● Give children their rhymes from Hour 2 to share with their partners. Encourage them to read their rhymes with expression and intonation, volume and rhythm.
● Ask them to work with their partners to create additional rhyming phrases for their rhymes. Let them refer to photocopiable page 68 for rhyming words.

Differentiation

Less able
● Work with this group to help develop their dramatisation of the whole rhyme.

More able
● Emphasise the need for the children to read their rhymes with expression.
● Additionally, try the activity described for less able children in Hour 2.

Plenary
● Choose two children to read their rhymes aloud.
● Pose questions to the other children such as: *Which particular part of the rhyme did you like best? Why? What was special about the words? What pictures did the words conjure in your minds? Which words made you think of that?*
● Include the children who read the rhymes in the discussion by asking them about their choice of words.
● Display the children's rhymes either on the wall or in a class book.
● Also provide an opportunity, possibly as part of an assembly, for the children to perform their drama to an audience.

The north wind doth blow

Objectives
T4: To read poems independently, to point while reading and make correspondence between words said and read.
T6: To recite stories and rhymes.
S2: To use awareness of the grammar of a sentence to decipher new or unfamiliar words.

What you need
● Photocopiable page 66, plus envelopes of the poem cut into strips
● a bag of rhyming word cards
● A4 sugar paper.

Shared text-level work
● Introduce the new rhyme, 'The north wind doth blow' to the children.
● As with the previous poem, recite it before displaying and reading the text.
● Invite the children to explain what the rhyme is about. Encourage them to describe the pictures in their minds and to further their imagination by exaggerating the 'bitterness' of the wind and snow and the plight of the poor robin.
● Ask questions to elicit understanding of difficult words such as *doth* and *barn*.
● Recite the rhyme again, but this time encourage the children to join in.
● Tell them that they are going to learn the rhyme by heart and help them to memorise it. Do this by reciting one line for children to repeat, then the next and so on.
● Finally recite the complete rhyme together.

Shared word-level work
● Display the rhyme and point to the words as you read. Do the same again, asking children to point to the words to demonstrate the correct match between words said and read.
● Encourage the children to explain the reading strategies they are using in order to read unfamiliar words.
● Ask the children to point to and say words that rhyme, for example *blow* and *snow*, *thing* and *wing*.
● Explain the subtle difference between *warm* and *barn* and that rhyming words sometimes don't quite match up as, for example, *dame* and *lane* in 'Baa baa black sheep'.
● Play the game the less able group played in Hour 2, asking for one rhyming word for each card.

Guided work
● Use the rhyme, if appropriate (if not, the graded reading book), to raise the children's awareness of and gain practice in strategies they use for reading new and unfamiliar words.

Independent work
● Give each pair of children an envelope containing the strips of the rhyme.
● Ask the pairs to read, sort and reassemble the rhyme in the correct order by sticking the strips on to coloured sugar paper.
● Tell the children then to read the rhyme to one another, using the intonations and appropriate volume that they practised in the shared session.

Plenary
● Ask the two more able groups to present their dramatisation of the rhyme to the rest of the class.

Differentiation
Less able
● Help the children to read the rhyme with appropriate expression and volume. Following this the children can illustrate the rhyme.

More able
● In two groups, ask children to act out the rhyme in the same way that 'Blow wind blow' was acted out in Hour 3.

Rhyming words

Objectives

NLS
S3: To draw on grammatical awareness, to read with appropriate expression and intonation.
T6: To recite rhymes with predictable and repeating patterns.
W1: To practise and secure the ability to rhyme.

S&L
9 Speaking: To interpret a text by reading aloud with some variety in pace and emphasis.

What you need
● Photocopiable page 66
● bags of rhyming word cards
● enlarged copies of photocopiable page 69.

Shared text-level work
● Begin the session by reciting 'The north wind doth blow'. Use plenty of expression, intonation and enjoyment.
● Recite the rhyme again, asking the children to recite it with you.
● Encourage the children to copy your expressions and intonation as you recite.
● Ask the children if they think they could recite the rhyme by themselves and give some children the opportunity to try this.
● If they have difficulty remembering the words, encourage other children to offer help as appropriate.
● Check that the children can remember the meanings of *doth* and *barn* from the previous session.

Shared word-level work
● Show the children the bag of word cards and remind them of the activity they played in the previous session.
● Tell them that this time, instead of providing just one rhyming word, whoever is chosen must pick a word and provide as many rhyming words as they can.
● Again, choose a child to pick and read a word from the bag.
● When the child has provided as many rhyming words as he or she can think of, they should choose a friend to pick a word from the bag have a go at the same activity.

Guided work
● Work with two groups to practise reading the poem with appropriate expression and intonation. Encourage the children to talk about the story and the rhythm of the poem to help them commit the poem to memory.

Independent work
● Organise the children into pairs and give each pair enlarged photocopiable page 69.
● Ask the children to cut out the words and work together to sort them into rhyming families according to the sets on the sheet.
● Ensure that the children discuss and make shared decisions about grouping the words.
● Encourage the children to add new rhyming words to the sets if they can and to write these on blank cards.

Plenary
● Ask the group learning the rhyme by heart (see Differentiation) to recite it for the rest of the class.
● After their recitation, ask the children in the group what helped them to learn the rhyme. *Did acting out the rhyme help you remember? Did the story help? What about rhythm?*
● Bring the session and unit to a close with a final recitation by the whole class.

Differentiation

Less able
● Help the children to learn the rhyme by heart so that they can recite it independently. Draw on dramatisation as in Hour 3 to assist recall.

More able
● Ask pairs to pick a word from the bag of cards and list rhyming words.
● Display the lists for use in future sessions on rhyme.

Wind poems

Blow wind blow
Blow wind blow!
And go mill go!
That the miller may grind his corn,
That the baker may take it
And into bread make it
And bring us some fresh in the morn.

The north wind doth blow
The north wind doth blow,
And we shall have snow,
And what will poor robin do then, poor thing?
He'll hide in a barn
To keep himself warm,
And hide his head under his wing, poor thing.

■SCHOLASTIC

Blow wind blow!

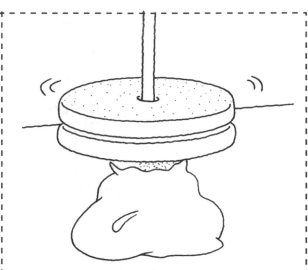

And go mill go!

That the miller may grind his corn,

That the baker may take it
And into bread make it

And bring us some fresh in the morn.

TERM 1

Rhyming spelling sort

go	blow	toe	grow
low	snow	know	hoe
flow	foe	so	show
no	crow	row	slow
glow	mow	sow	tow

◼SCHOLASTIC

Rhyming sets

■ Cut out the rhyming words and put them in the correct circles.

-ill

-ing

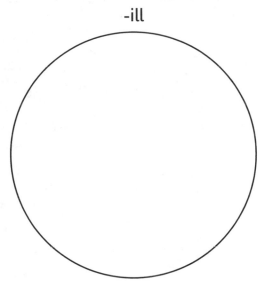

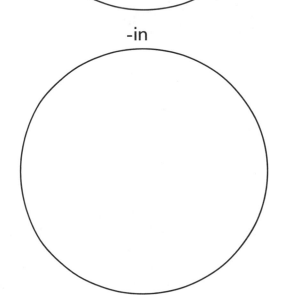

-ow

-in

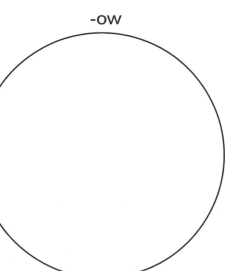

tin	hill	thing	crown	show
string	chin	will	sing	fin
blow	snow	mill	wing	bin

UNIT 6

Non-fiction 2

These sessions provide exciting practical activities for developing knowledge and understanding about lists and instructions. Simple traditional snacks from around the world provide a context for exploring the diversity of language. There are opportunities for cross-curricular links with geography, design and technology, PSHE and ICT. All the recipes promote healthy eating. In Hour 5, it is suggested that children eat sandwiches they have prepared. If you do this, you should follow school policy regarding children sampling food and ingredients, both in terms of cultural and religious restrictions as well as safety and allergies.

Hour	Shared text-level work	Shared word-/sentence-level work	Guided and independent work	Plenary
1 Brie and grape baguette	Following a recipe.	Exploring new words for spelling patterns.	Creating own baguette recipe.	Reading each other's recipes.
2 Sausage pumpernickel	Learning new words from another country; following another recipe.	Practising pronunciation of topic words.	Identifying topic verbs.	Pick out, read and say topic word cards.
3 Breads from around the world	Discussing what children know about different types of bread.	Labelling the breads, drawing upon word-level skills to read new words.	Listening to each other's experiences of eating breads.	Higher ability children tell their partners' experiences to the class.
4 Tortilla wrap	Following a recipe and applying word-level skills to read new words.	Following a recipe and applying word-level skills to read new words.	Creating their own sandwich recipe.	Children report about the photograph recipe they are making.
5 Name the sandwich	Reading one of the children's recipes.	Examining the collections of food words and 'what to do words' to explore letter patterns and sounds.	Reading recipes to follow instructions.	Sharing the sandwiches and discussing choices made and names given.

Key assessment opportunities

● Can the children read or listen to and follow simple instructions?

● Can they write simple instructions and captions?

● Have they learned new words?

Brie and grape baguette

Objectives

NLS
T13: To read and follow simple instructions.
T16: To write and draw simple instructions.
W12: To learn new words from reading and shared experiences, and to make collections of words linked to particular topics.

What you need
● A baguette, a small piece of brie, a few seedless white grapes
● a knife and board
● photocopiable page 76
● recipe instruction word cards, such as those on photocopiable page 78.

Shared-text level work
● Begin by setting the context for the unit. Tell the children that they are going to prepare food snacks from around the world.
● Find out what the children already know by asking them about the dishes they eat and where they come from.
● Move on to discussing recipes. Ask what you need to know in order to make pizza, a sandwich, a cake and so on. Establish the need for:

● ingredients – what it's made of
● equipment – what you use
● instructions – the steps to follow.

● Say that you are going to use a recipe to make an open sandwich. Display photocopiable page 76 and show the real ingredients and equipment in relation to the text.
● Ask the children to help you follow the recipe so you can make the sandwich. Notice the words like *split, slice, put* and *stick* that tell us what to do.

Shared word-level work
● Display the words *brie, baguette* and *grapes*. Explain that brie is a cheese from a place in France, that baguette is a type of French bread and that France is famous for growing grapes. The word grape also comes from the French language.
● Talk about other food words from France, such as *omelette, mayonnaise, quiche, meringue* and even *margarine*, and explore them in relation to the children's experience. Look at some of the peculiar spelling patterns, for example the soft g in *margarine*, the *-ette* in *baguette* and *omelette*, the *-gue* in *meringue*. Suggest that you make a class collection of food words from France.
● Place a large sheet of paper on the wall to be added to during the week (the running task). Write up the words from this Hour.
● Let parents know that the children are collecting French words related to food and watch the interest and motivation grow!

Differentiation

Less able
● Provide a writing frame similar to the brie and grape baguette recipe.

More able
● Focus the group on providing a clear and ordered set of picture/word instructions, but with their own ingredients. Encourage them to use their own instruction words.

Guided and independent work
● Ask the children to create their own recipe for an open baguette. Provide instruction word cards for each table.
● Remind the children that it is important to provide clear steps in the correct order so that another person can follow their instructions.
● Encourage the children to add to the list any useful words that they choose in their recipe.

Plenary
● Organise the children to sit with their talk partners. Ask the pairs to read each other's recipes and see if they can understand what to do.
● Choose a child to explain how to make their partner's sandwich by using his or her recipe.

📖 71

UNIT 6 HOUR 2 ▨ Non-fiction 2

Sausage pumpernickel

Objectives

NLS

T13: To read and follow simple instructions.
S2: To use awareness of the grammar of a sentence to decipher new or unfamiliar words.
W12: To learn new words from reading and shared experiences, and to make collections of words linked to particular topics.

What you need

● photocopiable pages 76–78
● pumpernickel bread, small portion of German sausage, tub of sauerkraut, tub of quark
● bread knife, flat knife, spoon, board
● 'Ingredients' picture cards taken from photocopiable pages 76 and 77
● a globe
● the class puppet
● recipe instruction word cards in a cloth bag.

Differentiation

Less able

● Provide a bag with the cards from photocopiable pages 76 and 77. One child is 'Keeper of the bag' while the others take turns to pick a card and say the word. The children should then swap roles.

More able

● With support, let children follow the recipe to make the pumpernickel sandwich. Make sure the children's hands are clean.

Shared text-level work

● Display the title of photocopiable page 77, 'Sausage pumpernickel', and explain to the children that you have another recipe from another country.
● Point to and say the word *pumpernickel* and enjoy the sound of the word with the children.
● Encourage the children to use grammar and context to identify what type of words these new ones are.
● Ask the children which country they think the word might be from.
● Show the children where Germany is on the globe and its relationship to the UK and France.
● Then show them the actual ingredients for this traditional German open sandwich.
● Show the children the entire recipe then, as in Hour 1, follow the recipe.
● Involve the children in reading the words and interpreting the pictorial instructions to help you make the sandwich.

Shared word-level work

● As in Hour 1, pick out the 'what to do' imperatives and choose children to demonstrate the actions of the words *slice, spread* and *spoon.*
● Look again at the recipe from Hour 1 and pick out the 'what to do' words. Ask different children to demonstrate these actions.
● Then look more closely at the spellings by playing 'Croaker', using a familiar class puppet.
● To play this game, choose a child to pick a word card from the bag and tell everyone what it is.
● The puppet (you) then pronounces it incorrectly, for example *spice* for *slice, thread* for *spread, stoon* for *spoon, flit* for *split, thick* for *stick, bash* for *mash.*
● Ask the children to point out the bit of the word the puppet keeps getting wrong.
● Tell the children that you now need two more large sheets of paper for word collections – one for food words from Germany and one for words that tell you what to do.

Guided and independent work

● Ask the children to complete photocopiable page 78 by selecting the correct words from those at the bottom of the page to write in the empty boxes.

Plenary

● Invite children from all ability groups to pick and read aloud word cards from the cloth bag.
● It would be exciting for the children to sample the unusual tastes of the sausage pumpernickel but, if you do this, you should follow school policy concerning eating food prepared in class.

Breads from around the world

Objectives

NLS
T12: To read and use captions, eg labels.
S4: To write captions and simple sentences.
W10: To recognise the critical features of words.

S&L
1 Speaking: To describe incidents or tell stories from their own experience.
2 Listening: To listen with sustained concentration.

What you need
● Selection of breads including baguette, pumpernickel, a traditional British loaf, naan, pitta, tortilla, bagel, chapatti, covered by a cloth
● label cards for the breads
● a globe.

Shared text-level work
● Remind the children about the baguette and pumpernickel sandwiches and read the words from the wall collections.
● Show the children a familiar loaf of bread but keep the other breads hidden by the cloth. Explain that the baguette and pumpernickel are types of bread.
● Write *bread* on the board, involving children with the sounds *b, r* and *d*, and spelling pattern *ea*.
● Ask about the different ways in which the children eat bread, for example sandwiches, bread and butter pudding, toast and breadcrumbs.
● Next turn attention to the other breads by removing the cloth. Choose one and ask the children if they can tell you what it is called or if they have ever eaten it.
● Explore when and where they have eaten it – at home, in restaurants or in another country; how they have eaten it, with what other foods and so on. Perhaps they have a special story to tell about eating bread? Tell your own anecdote if it helps to start things off.
● Establish the country with which the bread is associated and find the country on the globe. Describe its location in relation to the UK, France and Germany.
● Repeat this for each type of bread, giving the children a chance to share their experiences of eating it.

Shared word-level work
● Now that the names of the breads have been established suggest that it would be helpful to label the breads.
● Fix the card names of the breads to the board with Blu-Tack. Choose children to select and say the name on a card and place it next to the right bread.
● Ask each child to explain how they were able to read the word, for example ask *How did you know it said 'pitta'?* so that the children articulate some of the spelling strategies they are using to read words.
● Leave the bread and labels as a reference display.

Guided and independent work
● Organise the furniture so that the children can work quietly in pairs. Instruct the children to choose one of the breads to talk about, in a similar way to the shared session.
● Tell the children to listen carefully to each other. Emphasise that the task is about telling someone else's story, so they must listen intently.
● At about the midway point, organise for two pairs to join together where they each tell their friend's story about eating their chosen bread. (This is an ideal activity in which to involve parents who can encourage the children to be good listeners.)

Differentiation

Less able
● This group could work with the classroom assistant in a quiet area outside the classroom.

More able
● Tell the children that they should listen carefully to their partner's story so that they can tell it to the whole class in the plenary.

Plenary
● Establish a special area in the classroom for the higher ability group to share each other's stories with the rest of the class.

UNIT 6 HOUR 4 ☐ Non-fiction 2

Tortilla wrap

Objectives

NLS

T13: To read and follow simple instructions.
T15: To make simple lists.
T16: To write and draw simple instructions.
W12: To learn new words from reading and shared experiences, and to make collections of words linked to particular topics.

What you need

● A packet of tortillas, avocado, sour cream, carrots, spring onions, salsa, lettuce
● a knife and board, fork, teaspoons, bowl plate
● word cards for the ingredients for this recipe: *tortilla, avocado, sour cream, carrot, spring onion, salsa, lettuce*
● 'what to do' word cards for this recipe: *cut, remove, scoop, mash, spread, grate, spoon, shred, place, chop, sprinkle, fold*
● 'what to do' word cards from photocopiable page 78
● a digital camera.

Differentiation

Less able

● Organise for half of the group, with support, to make the tortilla wrap following the recipe on the board while the other half take photographs.

More able

● Organise for half the group to make the tortilla wrap while the other half observe and add words and pictures to the recipe on the board.

Shared text- and word-level work

● Attach the recipe words to the board in a jumbled fashion. Write *Ingredients* and *What to do* for the children to sort words later under the two headings.
● Say that you are going to make a tortilla wrap, using a tortilla that they looked at in Hour 3.
● Explain that as you make the wrap you will need their help to construct a recipe on the board.
● Show the children that at the moment all the 'ingredients' and 'what to do' words are muddled up but, as you make the wrap, they can help by putting the words in the right place and in the right order.
● Begin by placing the tortilla on the kitchen board and ask a child to find the word *tortilla*. Ask: *What's the first sound in 'tortilla'?* Then: *Can you see a word beginning with 't'?* And: *Can you see the two 'tall men' 'double ll' near the end of the word?* Guide the child in placing the *tortilla* card directly underneath *Ingredients*.
● Move on to *avocado*. Cut the avocado in half, choosing a child to find the word *cut* to place in the correct column. Continue to involve the children as you *remove* the stone and *scoop* out the flesh, *mash* it, *spread* it, then *spread* the *sour cream* on top. *Grate* the *carrot* and *spoon* some onto the tortilla. *Shred* the *lettuce* and *place* on top of the carrot. *Chop* the *spring onion* and *sprinkle* on top. *Fold* the sides and bottom of the tortilla around the food. Show the children why it is called a wrap.
● Examine the recipe on the board. Ask if there is enough information for others to make the wrap. Discuss how pictures can help to clarify instructions.
● Show how another Mexican ingredient, *salsa* can be spooned on to the tortilla.
● Explain that avocado is the main ingredient in another famous Mexican dip called guacamole.
● Add food words from Mexico to the running task.

Guided and independent work

● Organise the children to work in pairs to design a special sandwich recipe, drawing upon all their experiences in this unit.
● Tell them that they can only choose foods from those used in the previous sessions, but that they can combine them in different ways.
● Explain that they will have an opportunity to make their sandwiches in the following session.
● Provide the children with a sheet divided into two columns as on the board. Also provide additional 'what to do' words.
● Ask the children to write instructions where they can and to add diagrams.

Plenary

● Ask the less able group to report on the wrap-making and the photographs they took. Give each child an opportunity to recount their part in the process.

UNIT 6 HOUR 5 Non-fiction 2

Name the sandwich

Objectives

NLS

T13: To read and follow simple instructions.

S4: To write captions and simple sentences.

W8: To read on sight other familiar words.

W12: To learn new words from reading and shared experiences

What you need

● The children's recipes from the previous session, including one for shared work

● the necessary ingredients and equipment for the children to follow the recipes

● blank stand-up place cards

● a digital camera.

Differentiation

Less able

● Help the children to put together the words and photographs from the previous session. Ask them to assemble the recipe for wall display.

More able

● Let the children take photographs of children making sandwiches. Help them to choose and caption photographs to form a display.

Shared text-level work

● Organise the furniture so that pairs of children can work together comfortably.

● Place stand-up cards on the children's work places and organise their equipment and ingredients.

● Tell the children that all those who created recipes in the previous session will be using them in this session to make the sandwich.

● Display an enlarged version of one of the recipes created in Hour 4.

● Read with the children the list of ingredients and instructions, interpreting what to do from the words and helpful drawings.

● Focus on the ingredients the children have chosen and the country with which the foods are associated.

● Then ask the children to suggest a name for their sandwich. Encourage them to think about what name would reflect the food and its country of origin.

Shared word-level work

● Gather the children around the running task lists to see how they have grown and what words have been added.

● Choose children to share the additions they have made, explaining the meaning of the word and how they learned to spell it.

● Hopefully the collections will provide a variety of interesting foods and interesting words to explore, perhaps including *coq au vin, strudel* and *chilli con carne*.

● Let the children really enjoy the sounds in the words and the relationship of letter patterns and sounds.

Guided and independent work

● Organise the children in their pairs to follow their sandwich recipes. Ensure that all the children wash their hands.

● Provide as much adult support as possible, ensuring the adults support the children's independence rather than taking over the activity.

● Tell the pairs that they should try to complete their sandwiches so that they can be tasted in the plenary.

● Encourage them to discuss and agree on a name for their sandwich then to write it neatly on the stand-up card in front of them, asking for help with spelling where necessary.

Plenary

● Ask the children who have made sandwiches to invite other children to sample them.

● Draw the unit to a close by asking one or two pairs to talk about the ingredients they used and the country associated with them, how they went about making their sandwich and what name they gave it and why.

● If there is time, make a class list of the ingredients and 'what to do' words for one of the sandwiches and write a simple recipe.

Brie and grape baguette

Ingredients	What to do
baguette	split in half
brie	slice and put on baguette
grapes	slice and stick to brie

Sausage pumpernickel

Ingredients	What to do
pumpernickel	slice
quark	spread
sausage	slice
sauerkraut	spoon

Useful 'what to do' words

◼ Choose the correct label for each picture.

eat	mash	grate	slice	spoon	scoop
shred	split	stick	cut	spread	chop

UNIT 1

Narrative 1

This unit is based on two traditional stories taken from very different cultures. The first, 'Mr Polar Bear and the Hobyahs' is an adaptation of a traditional British folk story whereas 'The Greedy Guest' is a traditional folk tale from Dominica, with the character of Papa Bwa. During the unit, the children will role-play the characters and compare the two stories, drawing together universal folk themes about domestic settings, forests and strangers. In Hours 3 to 5, there are activities to meet *Progression in Phonics* Steps 5 to 7. Hour 6 ties in with 'Developing the concept of a sentence' in *Developing Early Writing*.

Hour	Shared text-level work	Shared word-/ sentence-level work	Guided work	Independent work	Plenary
1 Telling a traditional tale	Telling the story of Mr Polar Bear and the Hobyahs, establishing sequence of events.	Re-reading character names and using initial capital letters.	Using simplified text to read the story and interpret events and characters.	Placing pictures of story in sequence and re-telling the story.	Interactive retelling of story using felt board.
2 Comparing oral and written stories 💬	Noticing differences between written and spoken forms of storytelling.	Revising use of capital letters and full stops.	Using simplified text to read the story and interpret events and characters.	Making picture story books.	Discussing differences between written and told stories.
3 A traditional tale from Dominica	Telling the story of Papa Bwa, establishing the sequence of events.	Using the refrain from the story to focus on initial consonant cluster *cr*.	Using simplified text to read the story and interpret events and characters.	Placing pictures of story in sequence and re-telling the story.	Pairs tell a section of the story to the class.
4 Comparing the two stories	Comparing the two stories.	Discriminating between initial consonant clusters *br*, *cr*, and *tr*.	Re-reading stories to make comparisons.	Comparing the two stories.	Discussing similarities; reinforcing recognition of initial phoneme pairs.
5 Portraits	Discussing characters.	Identifying phonemes.	Painting and drawing a given character in discussion with other children and supportive adults.	Painting and drawing a given character in discussion with other children and supportive adults.	Talking about character portraits.

UNIT 1

Hour	Shared text level work	Shared word/ sentence level work	Guided work	Independent work	Plenary
6 Characters	Discussing characters and character portraits.	Writing a sentence to describe feelings about characters.	Writing a sentence to describe a character.	Writing a sentence to accompany their picture from previous session.	Revising sentence punctuation; displaying the captioned portraits.
7 Comparing endings	Comparing story endings; sharing opinions.	Writing different sentences to conclude stories.	Changing the ending of a story.	Changing the ending in simplified versions of a story.	Reinforcing the concept of a sentence; noticing similarities in story language for endings.
8 The Hobyahs 💬	Drama session role-playing Hobyahs.	Collecting new words from experience to describe the Hobyahs.	Writing descriptive sentences.	Drawing pictures of the Hobyahs; describing other children's pictures.	Discussing whether what has been written and said gives an accurate description.
9 Precious things	Relating the plot from 'Mr Polar Bear and the Hobyahs' to the children's experiences.	Writing a sentence related to a personal interpretation of the story.	Writing a sentence related to a personal interpretation of the story.	Writing a sentence related to a personal interpretation of the story.	Discussing precious possessions.
10 To the rescue 💬	Inventing characters to come to the rescue and frighten the Hobyahs away.	Writing a sentence based on the children's ideas of a character coming to their rescue.	Working together to draw and paint a picture of their character.	Working together to draw and paint a picture of their character.	Describing the special qualities of their characters.

Key assessment opportunities
● Can the children interpret a story through describing and explaining events, giving reasons for incidents?
● Can they describe the appearance, behaviour and qualities of characters?
● Can they role-play characters?
● Do they write in sentences, using capital letters and full stops?

Telling a traditional tale

Objectives

NLS
T4: To retell stories, giving the main points in sequence.
T7: To discuss reasons for, or causes of, incidents in stories.
S7: To use capital letters for names.

What you need

● Photocopiable pages 91 and 92
● cards from photocopiable pages 93 and 94
● small books made from photocopiable pages 93 and 94
● a felt/magnetic board or interactive whiteboard.

Shared text-level work

● Before the session, learn and rehearse the story of Mr Polar Bear and the Hobyahs in order to tell it to the children.
● Edit and embellish the text to suit yourself, so that in future sessions the children can discuss the differences between a told story and one that is read to them.
● Generate a storytelling atmosphere by creating a special area especially for telling stories. Playing some music or dimming the lights will signal to the children that a story is about to be told and encourage them to listen.
● Read and enjoy the story. Then help the children to recall the main points in sequence by asking:

● What was happening at the beginning of the story?
● Why were the little old man and the little old woman sad?
● Who was it who knocked at their door?
● How did the little old man feel?
● How did the little old woman feel?
● Why do you think she was reluctant to let him in?
● What would you have done?
● What happened next?

● Tell the children that they are going to use pictures to help them tell the story.

Shared sentence-level work

● Write the characters' names on the board and discuss spelling patterns so that the children will recognise them when reading.
● Also point out that names start with capital letters: Mr Polar Bear, Hobyahs, but not *little old man*, and *little old woman* because we are not told their names.

Guided work

● Use the small books to conduct guided reading with a focus on interpretation of the events and how the characters feel in response.

Differentiation

Less able
● Organise the group to take turns in placing the cards in sequence on a felt board or interactive whiteboard as they tell the story.

More able
● Ask the children to add text cards from photocopiable page 94 to their picture sequence.

Independent work

● Organise the children to work in pairs. Give each pair the eight pictures from photocopiable page 93 and ask them to arrange them in the correct sequence on their tabletop.
● Then ask the children to help each other retell the story so that they are familiar with the sequence of events and the reactions and responses of the characters.

Plenary

● Reinforce the children's understanding of the sequence of events and their ability to tell stories by using the felt storyboard as a prompt for interactive retelling.

UNIT 1 HOUR 2 ▢ Narrative 1

Comparing oral and written stories

Objectives

NLS
T4: To retell stories, giving the main points in sequence and to notice differences between written and spoken forms of retelling.
S4: To recognise full stops and capital letters when reading.

S&L
5 Speaking: To retell stories, ordering events using story language.

What you need
● A felt board
● photocopiable pages 93 and 94
● the small picture books
● sugar paper booklets.

Shared text-level work
● Use the felt board to display the first picture and corresponding text. Point to the text with a pointer as you read.
● Discuss how, in your storytelling, you were able to embellish the text by making additions or leaving things out.
● Cover the text and invite the children to tell their story version of the first picture in order to make the point that the telling of a story is slightly different every time.
● Do this for all eight pictures and text.

Shared sentence-level work
● Write the first sentence from the story on the board without using a capital letter or a full stop.
● Ask the children to identify what is wrong with the sentence and choose two children to write the capital letter and full stop in the correct place.
● Display the next sentence, using photocopiable page 94, and point out the capital letter and the full stop.
● Talk about it being a long sentence and show the children how the sentence makes sense by just reading *Every year... they would prepare for Christmas time* but that the middle bit tells us more about what time of year it is.
● Compare this with the sentence beginning *Soon they were...*, from the card beginning *Then the Hobyahs arrived,* again pointing out the length and the similar descriptive 'list'.
● Invite the children to point out the capital letter at the beginning of the sentence and the full stop at the end.

Guided work
● Read together as in Hour 1 with different groups.

Independent work
● Organise the children into talk partnerships.
● Give each pair blank sugar paper booklets in which to stick appropriate pictures and text in sequence from photocopiable pages 93 and 94.
● Advise them to create double-page spreads: one page for picture, facing page for corresponding text.

Differentiation

Less able
● Help the children to match the pictures and text.

More able
● Encourage the children to discuss in their pairs the differences between their told story from session 1 and the written version in their book?

Plenary
● Keep children seated at their tables and ask them to discuss the pictures and text in relation to their told stories.
● After about five minutes, choose some children to explain these differences. For example, in *telling,* the story can be embellished and the teller can address the audience by speaking directly to them but the written form remains the same.

A traditional tale from Dominica

Objectives

NLS

T4: To retell stories, giving the main points in sequence.

T7: To discuss reasons for, or causes of, incidents in stories

W3: To discriminate, read and spell words with initial consonant clusters.

What you need

- A globe
- a sun hat, flip-flops, sarong (if appropriate)
- Caribbean music
- photocopiable pages 95 and 96
- cards from photocopiable pages 97 and 98
- small books made from photocopiable pages 97 and 98.

Shared text-level work

- Tell the children that you are going to tell them another traditional story, this time from a far away country called Dominica.
- Show on a globe where Dominica is in relation to the UK.
- Set the scene for the story by talking briefly about the climate and culture of the Caribbean – some children may have been on holiday there or have relatives from there and could contribute their knowledge.
- Put on a sun hat, flip-flops and perhaps a sarong and play some Caribbean music, then tell the story.
- As in Hour 1, establish the main points and themes of the story by asking questions:

- What was happening at the beginning of the story?
- Why was Nana angry at her husband?
- What did Papa Bwa have to do before Nana would give him any dinner?
- What would you have thought if a guest at dinner began to eat the dishes?
- What might you have done?
- What happened when the woodcutter and Papa Bwa entered the forest?
- What would you have said to Papa Bwa?
- What might you have done?

- Tell the children that they are going to have another opportunity to tell the story using some pictures.

Shared word-level work

- Display the refrain from the story. Read it with the children:

Crick crack. I want it back.
I want my beard and that is that.

- Focus on the initial consonant cluster *cr*. Ask the children if they can think of any other words beginning with *cr* and collect their suggestions on a large sheet of paper, for example *crown, crunch, crackle, cracker, crinkle, crust, crush, creature.*
- Display the sheet on a wall for the children to add further examples.

Guided work

- Continue as Hour 1, with the new mini story books.

Independent work

- Repeat the activity from Hour 1, with photocopiable page 97.

Plenary

- Reinforce the children's understanding of the sequence of events and their ability to tell stories by choosing pairs of children to tell a section of the story to the other children in the class.

Differentiation

Less able

- Organise the group to take turns in placing the cards in sequence on a felt board or interactive whiteboard as they tell the story.

More able

- Ask the children to add text cards from photocopiable page 94 to their picture sequence.

Comparing the two stories

Objectives

NLS
T6: To identify and discuss a range of story themes, and to compare.
W3: To discriminate, read and spell words with initial consonant clusters.

What you need
● Paper bags
● cards from photocopiable page 99
● books made from photocopiable pages 93, 94, 97 and 98.

Shared text-level work
● Recall the two stories and tell the children that together you are going to explore things that are similar and things that are different.
● Draw a line down the board and write *Same* on one side and *Different* on the other. Discuss the stories and involve the children in deciding *Same* or *Different*. For example, *Do both stories have a husband and wife as main characters?* (Allow the children to explore that although we're not told that the little old man and little old woman are married we presume they are.) *How do you know Nana and the woodcutter are married?* Write *husband and wife* under *Same*.
● Ask what else is similar about the characters, for example where they live. (In a house near the forest.) *How does the wife feel about Mr Polar Bear or Papa Bwa being invited in?* (Neither the little old woman nor Nana want them in.) *What about Mr Polar Bear and Papa Bwa? Both want to go in the house, but are their reasons for wanting to go in different? What does Mr Polar Bear do when he is in the house? What does Papa Bwa do? Mr Polar Bear and Papa Bwa behave differently, but what about the Hobyahs? Who are they like?*
● Continue to raise questions like this. If some points are not quite the same make a middle section on the board for *Nearly the same.*

Shared word-level work
● Remind the children of the collection of words beginning with *cr* that they made in the previous session.
● Write *br, cr,* and *tr* in large lower-case letters on three paper bags and attach them to the board. Show the three bags and ask volunteers to say each sound.
● Place the cards face down on the floor or your desk and choose children to pick a card, read the word and place it in the correct bag.

Guided work
● Work with two groups to read the stories with a focus on making comparisons between the two stories.

Independent work
● Give each pair of children a sheet of A3 paper. Tell them to draw and write similarities between the stories on one side and differences on the other, using the middle for those things that are nearly the same.
● Ask them to write *Same, Nearly the same* and *Different* at the top of their sheet.

Differentiation

Less able
● Let children use one-word labels or short phrases to list similarities and differences.

More able
● Expect more written explanation of similarities and differences.

Plenary
● Choose pairs of children to share their ideas about what things they think are the same, nearly the same and different in the stories.
● Conclude the session by jumbling the *cr, br* and *tr* words in a cloth bag. Appoint one child to hold the bag who then chooses someone to pick a card and read it. If it is read correctly that child then holds the bag and chooses someone else to pick and read a card.

Portraits

Objectives

NLS
T8: To identify and discuss characters, eg appearance, behaviour, qualities.
W3: To discriminate, read and spell words with initial consonant clusters; to identify separate phonemes within words containing clusters.

S&L
7 Group discussion and interaction: To take turns to speak, listen to others' suggestions and talk about what they are going to do.

What you need
● Drawing and painting materials
● photocopiable page 99.

Shared text-level work
● Tell the children that you want them to think about the characters in the two stories.
● First, identify all the main characters and write their names on the board.
● With the children, pick one of the characters and explore his or her appearance, behaviour and characteristics.
● Encourage the children to tell you how they know the details about the features they suggest.
● Ask the children that if they were asked to draw or paint a picture of the character how would they capture all the qualities they have talked about.
● For example, *Would you paint him with kind eyes or cruel eyes, with a smile or a frown, colourful clothes or drab clothes? What might they be wearing or carrying?*
● Tell the children that they will be drawing or painting a character and trying to capture his or her characteristics.

Shared word-level work
● Write on the board the word *crick* from the refrain in 'The greedy guest' and draw sound buttons representing the phonemes underneath it. (See *Progression in Phonics*.)
● Do the same with other words from photocopiable page 99, for example:

c r ow n	t r ee	b r ea d	t r ai n
* * * *	* * *	* * * *	* * * *

● Ask the children to press a button and say the phoneme, then say the whole word.

Guided and independent work
● Organise the classroom into areas delineated by the characters in the story: little old man area, little old woman area, Mr Polar Bear area, Hobyahs area, Papa Bwa area and Whistling Bird area. Organise small groups of children to draw and paint their character.
● Encourage the children to discuss with adults and amongst themselves the characteristics of their figure, why they think this about them and how they are going to achieve a representation of it.

Differentiation

Less able
● Encourage extra talk with adults to help transfer ideas to pictorial representation.

More able
● Provide tape recorders so that children can record and play back their discussions about the characters.

Plenary
● Choose two portraits of different characters for the artists to talk about. Encourage them to explain the decisions they made about how they represented certain characteristics and features. Compare them with paintings of the same characters by other children and what features they chose to represent.
● Tell the children that in the next session you will be helping them to write about their picture.

UNIT 1 HOUR 6 ◾ Narrative 1

Characters

Objectives

NLS

T15: To build simple profiles of characters from stories read, describing characteristics, appearances, behaviour with pictures, single words, captions and sentences.
S5: To continue demarcating sentences in writing, ending a sentence with a full stop.
S7: To use capital letters for the personal pronoun *I*, for names and for the start of a sentence.

Shared text-level work

● Display two portraits of the same character painted in the previous session.
● Play any tape recording of the children's discussions.
● Decide with the children on a sentence that captures a particular characteristic of the figure from the story. Encourage the portrait artists and children on the tape to lead this discussion. Challenge the children to give reasons for the choices they make by drawing upon evidence from the story, for example:

> I thought the little old woman was mean because she didn't want Mr Polar Bear to come in.
> The whistling bird was kind because it helped the woodcutter and clever because he tricked the three wise women.

● Draw children's attention to the words they are choosing to describe their character, for example *mean, kind, clever*. Write these words on cards, along with the characters' names.
● Continue to identify characteristics and choose an appropriate sentence to model writing the sentence.

Shared sentence-level work

● Model writing the sentence by talking the children through decisions you make for the sentence to sound right and make sense. Draw upon the phonological and graphical knowledge cues and the children's sight vocabulary to spell words accurately.
● Reinforce children's understanding about when to use capital letters and full stops.

Guided work

● Work with two groups to compose a sentence that describes one of the characters, supporting children through discussion and modelling writing as in the shared session.

Independent work

● Tell the children to write their own sentence that describes their character to accompany their portrait from the previous session.
● Provide cards on which are written characters' names and useful words such as *mean, kind, clever, nasty, greedy, worried*.

Plenary

● Reinforce the process of composing a sentence by choosing two children to read their sentences and to explain their thinking.
● Write one of the sentences, unpunctuated, on the board and ask another child to correct it with capital letters and a full stop.
● Assemble the portraits and accompanying sentences to form a display in the classroom.

Differentiation

Less able
● Children should discuss their characters with the classroom assistant to determine one or two characteristics and then provide a one- or two-word caption.

More able
● Let children listen to their discussions from the previous session in order to choose one or two sentences to write.

Objectives

NLS
T10: To identify and compare basic story elements, eg endings in different stories.
T16: To use some of the elements of stories to structure own writing.
S5: To continue demarcating sentences in writing.

What you need

● Photocopiable pages 91, 92, 93 and 94
● The mini-books of the stories

Comparing endings

Shared text-level work

● Retell the stories from where Mr Polar Bear frightens off the Hobyahs and the whistling bird distracts Papa Bwa and the old women so that the woodcutter can escape.
● Lead a discussion about the similarities and differences in the endings by asking:

> ● Where were the little old man and the little old woman at the end of the story?
> ● Where were Nana and the woodcutter?
> ● Where were they when they were all safe? (Establish the home as a refuge.)
> ● Who were the helpers in both stories?
> ● How did they help?
> ● What did they do? (Establish animals helping humans.)

● Note that the stories both end with the 'problem' being resolved. Ask the children if they liked the endings. Would they change anything?

Shared sentence-level work

● Demonstrate writing a conclusion for one of the stories that is different from the original version, for example:

> Papa Bwa was so happy to be back in the forest listening to the whistling bird that he forgot all about the woodcutter.
> The Hobyahs thought they had escaped up the chimney but Mr Polar Bear chased after them and when he caught them he made them promise never to come back.

● Through a brief discussion, establish what the final sentence should be and demonstrate writing the sentence.

Guided work

● Work with two groups to write a conclusion to one of the stories. Encourage the children to make it different from the original.

Independent work

● Tell the children that they are going to make an additional back page for their little books that provides a different ending to the story. Provide appropriate sized paper so that the endings can be added to the books using a strip of adhesive tape.
● Encourage the children to write a concluding sentence of their choice.

Differentiation

Less able
● Ask the children to share their ideas but let an adult scribe.

More able
● Encourage the children to write more than one sentence.

Plenary

● Reinforce the process of composing a sentence by choosing two children to read their sentences and explain their thinking.
● Notice any frequently used phrases in the endings, such as *happily ever after* or *they ran and ran and ran as far away as they could*. Ask the children if they have heard phrases like this before in other stories.

The Hobyahs

Shared text-level work

● Organise a space for the children to take part in a drama session.
● Ask the children what they can remember about the Hobyahs and how they can describe them. Read the description from the story on photocopiable page 91 – *nasty little things, all gangly limbed and goggly eyed, with long licking tongues and sharp gnashing teeth…*
● Retell the part of the story where the Hobyahs come down the chimney and smash their way through the house eating up everything in sight. Tell the children that they are going to pretend to be Hobyahs.
● Use each part of the description in a step-by-step fashion, allowing the children to build up their dramatisation of the Hobyahs:

1. nasty little things
2. gangly limbed
3. goggly eyed
4. long licking tongues
5. sharp gnashing teeth.

● At each new part of the description, allow the children time to explore being and showing themselves as a *nasty little thing, gangly limbed* and so on.
● If there is time, continue the role-playing with the description *impolite little creatures smashing pots… sitting in the butter!*

Shared word-level work

● Ask the children if they learned anything else about the Hobyahs by role-playing them. Focus the discussion to elaborate on the text's description of the Hobyahs.
● Collect the children's ideas on the board. Begin by exploring the words *gangly* (to describe their limbs) and *goggly* (to describe their eyes). Ask the children to think of words to describe their fingers, toes, noses and hair, for example clawing, wriggly, pointy, knotty.
● As you list the words, draw upon the children's phonological and graphic knowledge to spell the words accurately.

Guided work

● Work in a group to compose descriptive sentences about the Hobyahs. Encourage the children to draw on their drama work.

Independent work

● Organise the children into pairs where they can't see each other's work. Ask each child to create a picture of a Hobyah.
● Then ask the pairs to exchange pictures and orally describe to their partner what they see in front of them. Remind them to describe the paintings using some of the words they learned earlier.

Plenary

● Share the pictures and written descriptions. Ask individual children if they think that what has been said and written gives accurate descriptions of the Hobyahs.

Precious things

Objectives

NLS
T14: To represent outlines of story plots, eg to make own version.
T16: To use some of the elements of known stories to structure own writing.
S5: To continue demarcating sentences in writing, ending a sentence with a full stop.

Shared text-level work

● Recap with the children the damage the Hobyahs caused in the house of the little old man and little old woman and write the following extract on the board:

> They would come down the chimney one after another, smashing their way through all the house, eating up everything that the little old man and the litttle old woman has prepared for Christmas.

● Ask the children to imagine that the Hobyahs are breaking into their homes and heading straight for their bedrooms!
● Then ask the children which of their things they would especially not want the Hobyahs to take or break. Which are their most special items? Encourage them to think about items that they have owned for a long time as well as, for example, recent Christmas presents. Perhaps there are items that the children have had since they were babies, such as a special teddy bear?
● Collect the children's ideas on the board.
● Encourage the children to explain why a particular thing is precious and why they would not want the Hobyahs to take or break.
● Ask questions such as: *When did you get it? Where? Who gave it to you? What does it mean to you? Do you link it to a happy time or place? Is it pretty? Does it feel nice?*

Shared sentence-level work

● Choose one of the children's ideas in order to demonstrate writing a sentence.
● Talk through your thinking regarding decisions you are making for the sentence to sound right and make sense.
● Provide the children with a sentence starter such as *I would not want the Hobyahs to damage my... because...*
● Reinforce the children's understanding about when to use capital letters and full stops.

Guided and independent work

● Ask the children to write their own sentence about what they would not want the Hobyahs to break or damage in their house.
● Provide a sentence starter as in the shared session on card for the children to adapt or complete.

Differentiation

Less able
● Encourage children to tape record their descriptions of their precious object.

More able
● Provide additional sentence starters on card that use *eat and steal* in place of *break* for children to complete.

Plenary

● Hold a discussion to find out what are the most precious possessions and why.
● Display some of the sentences alongside work from the previous session.
● Ask the children if they would like to bring their favourite item to school to be photographed or bring a photograph of the item so that it could be added to the display.

UNIT 1 HOUR 10 ▢ Narrative 1

To the rescue

Objectives

NLS

T14: To represent outlines of story plots, e.g. to make own version.
T16: To use some of the elements of known stories to structure own writing.
S5: To continue demarcating sentences in writing, ending a sentence with a full stop.

S&L

7 Group discussion and interaction: To take turns to speak, listen to others' suggestions and talk about what they are going to do.

What you need
● An enlarged version of one of the children's sentences from Hour 9
● drawing and painting materials.

Shared text-level work
● Remind the children of their ideas from the previous session: the favourite possessions they would not want the Hobyahs to take or break.
● Display an enlarged version of one of the children's sentences and read it with the whole class. Encourage a volunteer to point to the words as they are read.
● Now lead the children in a discussion about what animal they would most like to come to their rescue if the Hobyahs invaded their home, such as Mr Polar Bear or the whistling bird.
● List the children's ideas down the right-hand side of the board, encouraging those who make suggestions to indicate why that animal would be a good choice for scaring off the Hobyahs. For example, an lion might be a good choice because it has a loud roar; a tiger might be good because everyone is frightened of tigers.
● Now ask the children to provide words that add description. Give the example of the *whistling* bird, and others such as *terrifying* tiger, *roaring* lion, *trampling* elephant.
● Add the ideas on the left-hand side of the board, but do not match the descriptive words to the animals so that the children can make their own decisions about this.

Shared sentence-level work
● Choose with the children a combination of adjective and noun from the board and demonstrate writing a sentence linked to the story and the children's sentences in the previous session. For example, *A terrifying tiger leapt on the Hobyahs and scared them away; I asked a roaring lion to frighten the Hobyahs away.*

Guided and independent work
● Organise the children to work in partnerships of a good writer and a good artist, where possible.
● Ask the pairs of children to discuss and decide together which creature will save their favourite possession from the Hobyahs.
● Ask the artist to create a picture of their animal for the writer to describe in a sentence.
● Remind them to share ideas and agree on characteristics and a name before they begin.
● Suggest that the artist checks the writer's sentence for correct spellings and use of a capital letter and full stop.
● Listen to some of the children's discussions as you move around the groups.

Differentiation

Less able
● Ask the children to write a simple caption, such as *terrifying tiger*.

More able
● Challenge the children to write another sentence about *how* their animal prevented the Hobyahs from breaking their favourite possession.

Plenary
● Ask the pairs to present their paintings to the class and describe what special qualities their animal has that made them choose it to defend them against the Hobyahs.
● Display the paintings and descriptions.

Mr Polar Bear and the Hobyahs (1)

Once upon a time there lived a little old man and a little old woman. Every year when the winds were getting stronger, the days colder and shorter, the nights longer and darker, they would prepare for Christmas time.

The little old man and the little old woman would make pots of jam and chutney. They would bottle fruit and hang hams, game, salt bacon and beef. They would make cheese and butter, store nuts and dry fruit and, as Christmas neared, bake bread, pies, cakes and biscuits. But they did all this with sad eyes and a sad heart. You may well ask why.

You see, every Christmas Eve when most people are joyful at the thought of waking up to lots of presents, the little old man and the little old woman would lie half asleep, half awake, waiting for the Hobyahs to come.

The Hobyahs are nasty little things, all gangly limbed and goggly eyed, with long, licking tongues and sharp, gnashing teeth. They would come down the chimney one after another, smashing their way through all the house, eating up everything that the little old man and the little old woman had prepared for Christmas.

One year, just before Christmas, the little old man and the little old woman heard a knock at the door. No one ever called in the winter as the weather was at its most bitter, and the little old man and the little old woman lived many, many miles from anyone.

The little old man looked out of the snowed-up window and saw a huge polar bear knocking at the door. The little old man and the little old woman were afraid and shouted at the polar bear to go away but the polar bear pleaded to come in because he was so very cold.

"This is the coldest winter I have ever known" said Mr Polar Bear. "Please let me come in or I may die of frost bite."

TERM 2

Mr Polar Bear and the Hobyahs (2)

The little old woman still didn't want to invite the polar bear in. "He'll eat all our food just like the Hobyahs," she said, but the little old man persuaded her to let the polar bear in for fear he would die in the cold. Anyway, what was there to lose whether it was the polar bear or the Hobyahs who ate their food?

The polar bear was so tired that all he wanted to do was to rest by the fire with a bowl of milk by his head. The little old man gave him a bowl of warm milk. While the little old woman said, "Don't spill it!" Mr Polar Bear fell fast asleep like a great big rug in front of the dying fire.

As midnight passed, a speck of soot fell on to Mr Polar Bear's nose, quickly followed by the little claw-like feet of the first of the Hobyahs. Soon another, then another, jumped on to Mr Polar Bear's nose as they scrambled towards the feast of food the little old man and the little old woman had prepared for Christmas.

Mr Polar Bear twitched and raised his paw to scratch his nose. First he opened one eye then both eyes and saw these impolite little creatures smashing pots and licking their long tongues around the jars of jam.

Soon the Hobyahs were everywhere, tearing at the hams, gobbling up the cakes, stuffing their mouths with cheese and chutney, jam and marmalade and sitting in the butter!

Mr Polar Bear was not at all pleased at their behaviour, so with one giant move he rose up on his hind legs and roared a mighty bear roar. Needless to say the Hobyahs ran, jumped, bumped and scuttled in fright. Then they clawed and scratched one another as they jostled in their haste to get back up the chimney.

When the commotion was over, the little old man and the little old woman came downstairs to find the polar bear asleep again in front of the fire. The damage wasn't as bad as other years so they set to putting it right straight away.

Next day, at Christmas Hour, the little old man and the little old woman and the polar bear enjoyed a great feast of food.

That night the Hobyahs returned to peek in at the window to see if Mr Polar Bear was still there. He was there all right! Just as they were peeking through the window he stretched himself and yawned. Without waiting to see anymore the Hobyahs ran as far away as their horrible little legs would take them, never to return again to bother the little old man and the little old woman who lived happily ever after.

Mr Polar Bear and the Hobyahs (pictures)

Mr Polar Bear and the Hobyahs (text)

Once upon a time there lived a little old man and a little old woman. Every year when the winds were getting stronger, the days colder and shorter, the nights longer and darker, they would prepare for Christmas.

One year just before Christmas the little old man and the little old woman heard a knock at the door. "This is the coldest winter I have ever known," said Mr Polar Bear. "Please let me come in or I may die of frost bite."

The little old woman wasn't sure, but finally the little old man let him in and gave him a bowl of warm milk. The little old woman said, "Don't spill it!"

Then the Hobyahs arrived. Soon they were everywhere, tearing at the hams, gobbling up the cakes, stuffing their mouths with cheese and chutney, jam and marmalade and sitting in the butter!

Mr Polar Bear was not at all pleased at their behaviour, so with one giant move he rose up on his hind legs and roared a mighty bear roar.

Next day, at Christmas Hour, the little old man and the little old woman and Mr Polar Bear enjoyed a great feast of food.

That night the Hobyahs returned to see if Mr Polar Bear was still there. He was there all right!

The Hobyahs ran as far as their horrible little legs would take them, never to return again to bother the little old man and the little old woman who lived happily ever after.

The Greedy Guest (1)

One day, in the forest, a woodcutter met a strange old man. His hair was thick and tangled. His long bushy beard almost touched the ground. The woodcutter, who was very kind, invited the old man home to dinner. "This is Papa Bwa," he said to his wife Nana. "He says he is the guardian of the woods and very hungry."

Nana looked the old man up and down and said: "He'll have to wash and change into something cleaner." She pointed to a tub of water in the yard and gave him a pair of clean overalls. After he had washed and changed Nana was still unhappy.

"Man, this dirty beard has got to go if you want any dinner tonight." So Papa Bwa had to agree to have his beard shaved clean off. After dinner he curled up on a sofa and went to sleep.

A strange thing happened at breakfast the next morning. When Nana gave Papa Bwa a mug of tea, he drank the tea and ate the mug. At lunchtime he ate fried fish and plantains, then devoured the empty dish. When she gave him crab meat and calaloo, Papa Bwa polished off the plate as well. In fact, he ate his way through several plates, jugs, a calabash, a washing-up bowl and even a pig's trough.

Nana was very upset. She said to her husband: "You must take this creature back to the woods where you found him. If he goes on like this he will eat everything in our house

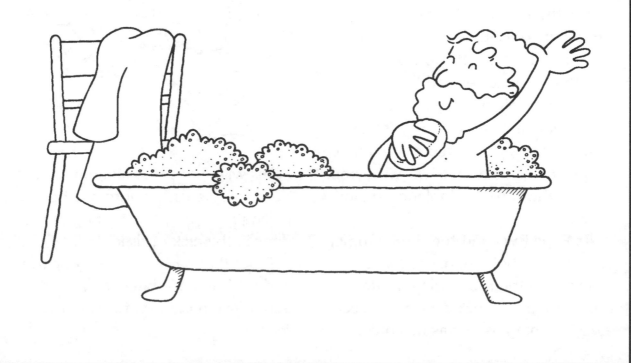

TERM 2

The Greedy Guest (2)

and what's to stop him eating us up as well?"

So the woodcutter led Papa Bwa back to the woods where they had met. There the old man suddenly started jumping up and down shouting:

Crick, crack, break my back
I want my beard, I want it back!
But his beard had been thrown on to a rubbish dump. What was the woodcutter to do?

Out of the blue appeared three wise women of the woods. They were curious to know what the racket was all about. The woodcutter explained.

The wise old women found it all rather funny and they too joined Papa Bwa chanting and dancing round the poor woodcutter until he was quite dizzy.

Just then a beautiful bird, a mountain whistler, swooped down from the treetops. It too was curious and the woodcutter had to tell the whole story all over again. Luckily the mountain whistler felt sorry for the woodcutter and wanted to help him.

"I will whistle a tune," it whispered. "When they are not looking, run for it, man."

As Papa Bwa and the three women whirled and twirled, danced and pranced to the mountain whistler's merry tune, the woodcutter slipped away, running as fast as he could.

His wife Nana was standing in the doorway. He rushed into the house, pulling her along and bolting the door in the nick of time.

From that day on, the woodcutter and his wife have been very careful about inviting guests to dinner.
Jane Grell

The Greedy Guest (pictures)

TERM 2

The Greedy Guest (text)

The woodcutter, who was very kind, invited the old man home to dinner.	Nana said: "He'll have to wash and change into something cleaner."
"Man, this dirty beard has got to go if you want any dinner tonight."	When Nana gave Papa Bwa crab mean and calaloo, he polished off the plate as well.
Crick, crack, break my back. I want my beard, I want it back!	The wise old woman joined Papa Bwa chanting and dancing round the poor woodcutter.
As Papa Bwa and the three women danced to the mountain whister's merry tune, the woodcutter slipped away.	Nana was standing in the door way. He rushed into the house, pulling her along and bolting the door in the nick of time.

■SCHOLASTIC

Consonant clusters

truck	**cream**	**brook**
crocodile	**tractor**	**trowel**
brick	**tree**	**treasure**
bride	**crane**	**bridge**
crown	**brush**	**bread**
crab	**train**	**crow**

UNIT 2

Non-fiction 1

The non-fiction book that this unit is based on *A Seed in Need* by Sam Godwin (Hodder) falls into a category of books often described as information texts, many of which use the question-and-answer format. The book provides a bridge between children's existing knowledge and understanding of stories and factual and systematically organised information books. Other books that may be used as alternatives are *The Drop Goes Plop* by Sam Godwin (Hodder), *Duck (Watch It Grow)* and *Snail (Watch It Grow)*, both by Barrie Watts (Franklin Watts).

Hour	Shared text-level work	Shared word-/ sentence-level work	Guided work	Independent work	Plenary
1 Non-fiction books	Introducing a non-fiction book.	Writing questions.	Writing a questions for the project.	Posing questions for the project and writing down the most important.	Choosing questions; deciding the next step.
2 Questions and answers	Reading, asking and answering questions.	Reading, asking and answering questions.	Suggesting and writing answers.	Providing drawings and simple written responses.	Small group discussion leading to collecting suggestions.
3 Useful words	Locating 'useful words' pages and glossaries in non-fiction books.	Putting key words in alphabetical order.	Compiling useful word pages for the class book.	Sorting suggestions for useful words page and arranging them alphabetically.	Reading the useful words pages in the class book.
4 Labelling	Looking at labelled diagrams.	Practical activity of labelling resources.	Reading labelled diagrams and discussing layout.	Making a labelled picture of things needed for planting seeds.	Reading the new page in the class book.
5 Planting seeds	Sorting photographs to show process of planting seeds.	Reinforcing questions and responses in sentences.	Planting seeds; discussing and photographing the process. Enjoy reading the completed class book.	Planting seeds; discussing and photographing the process.	Enjoy reading the completed class book.

Key assessment opportunities
● Can the children distinguish between fiction and non-fiction books, discussing layout and contents?
● Can they pose, write and respond to questions?
● Can they label diagrams?
● Have they learned new words from reading and experience of the topic?

NLS
T17: To use terms *fiction* and *non-fiction*, noting some of their differing features, eg layout.
T19: To predict what a given book might be about from a brief look at both front and back covers.
T24: To write simple questions.

S&L
7 Group discussion and interaction: To take turns to speak, listen to others' suggestions.

What you need
● *A Seed in Need* or other non-fiction book on seeds and plants/flowers
● a blank class Big Book made from folded sugar paper
● tape recorders.

Non-fiction books

Shared text-level work
● Begin by showing the children the book. Ask them to predict what it might be about by looking closely at the cover. Read the title and ask if it gives a further clue.
● Turn to the first double-page spread. Look at the layout and text. The question posed, *What does a seed need to make it grow?*, will reinforce the children's ideas about the subject of the book (and the answers inside will confirm them).
● Also read the sentences running along the bottom of the page (if appropriate) and establish that there are two sources of information.
● Turn the page and again examine the layout and text. Ask if this book is like a story. Continue to make comparisons between this book and story books.
● Explain that we use the word *fiction* for story books and *non-fiction* (*non* meaning *not*) for factual books.
● Read the book to enjoy the question and answer repartee.
● Introduce the idea of growing plants in the classroom and making a class information book about this.

Shared sentence-level work
● Return to the first page and notice how the book begins with a question. Ask: *What seeds would be good to grow in the classroom?*
● Write the question on the board and tell the children that you are using a question mark to show that the sentence is asking a question.
● Ask the children to suggest more questions for the project. For example, *Can we grow potatoes? Where shall we put the plant pots?*
● Tell the children that their questions could form the layout of a class book like *A Seed in Need*. Let the children talk with their partners about questions they would like to ask.

Guided work
● Work with a group to discuss and write questions the children want to use in their class book.

Independent work
● Organise the children to be with their talk partners. Ask them to listen to each other's suggested questions. Tell them that they cannot write them all down, so they are to decide which question is very important and write it down.

Differentiation

Less able
● Provide tape recorders for pairs to record their questions.

More able
● Support the children in a large group to begin to sort their questions into groups.

Plenary
● Share some of the questions and decide which the children want to include, which questions could sound better and which might be suitable for the first page of the class book. Stick or write the chosen question into the class Big Book.
● Come to a shared decision about the next step in the process. Suggest that the best seeds to choose should be fast-growing seeds like mustard, cress or beansprouts.

Questions and answers

Objectives

NLS

T12: Through shared writing to apply phonological, graphic knowledge and sight vocabulary to spell words accurately.

S6: To use the term *sentence* appropriately to identify sentences in text.

S&L

7 Group discussion and interaction: To take turns to speak, listen to others' suggestions and talk about what they are going to do.

What you need

● *A Seed in Need* or other chosen book.

Shared text- and sentence-level work

● Remind the children that they are going to grow plants from seeds and make their own class book about this.

● Write the question from Hour 1 on the board: *What seeds would be good to grow in the classroom?*

● Read other questions asked in the book. Hand the book to different children for them to locate and read out the questions.

● Tell the children that they need to raise similar questions about planting seeds and growing plants. For example, you want to know what equipment is needed because you have to get the items for the classroom.

● Demonstrate composing the question *What things do we need to plant seeds?* Model the writing, drawing upon children's phonological, graphic knowledge and sight vocabulary to spell words.

● Encourage the children to suggest answers for example, *plant pot*, *trowel*, *compost*.

● Now go back to the first question, *What seeds would be good to grow in the classroom?* Involve the children in composing the response sentence. Remind them of the suggestion made in the previous plenary to grow mustard, cress or beansprouts because they grow quickly. The sentence could be *Mustard, cress and beansprouts would be good because they grow quickly.*

● Proceed to compose the sentence with the children, involving them in the spelling and grammar.

● Recall the question and answer format in the book and read the question and answer together from the board: *What seeds would be good to grow in the classroom? Mustard, cress and beansprouts would be good because they grow quickly.*

Guided work

● Work with a group to discuss and write possible answers to the question on the board, *What things do we need to plant seeds?*

Independent work

● Ensure that the children can see the question on the board. Also provide the question on cards so that the children can see it at their tables.

● Ask the children to work with their talk partners to discuss what is needed to plant seeds in the classroom and record their suggestions in drawings and simple one- or two-word captions/labels.

Differentiation

Less able

● Organise pairs so that good writers can work with less able children.

More able

● Encourage the children to write in sentences.

Plenary

● Ask each pair to join up with another pair and, using their drawings and captions, discuss suggestions for the equipment and resources they will need for planting seeds.

● Bring the session to an end by choosing one or two children to say what their group have decided upon and write their suggestions up on the board to be used in the following session.

Useful words

What you need
● *A Seed in Need* or other chosen book
● the children's work from Hour 2.

Shared text-level work
● Organise the children so that they are with their talk partners.
● Begin by saying that you have looked at their suggestions from yesterday's session about what we need to plant seeds.
● Praise them for thinking of so many useful things.
● Tell the children that in *A Seed in Need* there is a page called 'Useful words' and that you think it would be a good idea to have such a page in their class book.
● Involve the children in locating the 'Useful words' page and choose a child to turn to the same place in the blank class book.
● Choose another child to write *Useful words* at the top of the page in the class book.
● Move swiftly on to word-level work to develop the 'Useful words' page together.

Shared word-level work
● Look at the 'Useful words' page in *A Seed in Need* and ask the children if they notice anything special about how the words are arranged.
● Refer to other glossaries and establish that they are arranged in alphabetical order. Ask the children why they think this is.
● Next, hand out the children's suggestions from Hour 1 and work together to provide a comprehensive list of words.
● You may find you have a very mixed collection of suggestions, such as *plant pots, sunshine, seeds, water, compost, trowel, plant pot saucer*, so take the opportunity to sort the words into groups to make more than one useful words page. You could, for example, have one page for *Things we need to plant seeds* and another for *Things the seeds need to grow*.
● Once you have decided about what words are to go on what page, involve the children in sorting them alphabetically.

Differentiation

Less able
● The main focus should be on sorting the words into alphabetical order. Ask the children to write the first letter of the word if they cannot spell the whole word.

More able
● Ask pairs to collaborate to make decisions about what useful word pages to construct and give a title for each page, such as *equipment* or *tools; what seeds need to grow*, listing their words alphabetically.

Guided work
● Work with two groups of children for compiling the useful words pages in the class book in alphabetical order.

Independent work
● Organise the children to work with the same talk partners as in Hour 2.
● Ask the pairs to sort their suggestions from the previous session to make useful words page(s) and then sort the words into alphabetical order.

Plenary
● Read the useful words pages in the class book that children in the guided writing groups have compiled.
● Tell the children that you will use the list for gathering together the things you will need to plant the seeds in the next session.

UNIT 2 HOUR 4 ☐ Non-fiction 1

Labelling

Objectives

NLS

T17: To use terms *fiction* and *non-fiction*, noting some of their differing features, e.g. layout, titles, use of pictures, labelled diagrams.
T22: To write labels for drawings and diagrams.
T23: To produce extended captions, eg to describe artefacts.
W11: To practise handwriting in conjunction with spelling and independent writing.

What you need

● *A Seed in Need* or other chosen book
● a selection of information books
● items for planting seeds: a plant pot, plant pot saucer, compost, margarine tub, seeds, bottle top, a watering can, a sticky label
● string.

Differentiation

Less able
● Help the children to create a page for the back of the class book that involves drawing resources and writing labels as in the shared writing session.

More able
● Challenge the children to provide additional information on the labels.

Shared text- and word-level work

● Show the children the page headed *The Sunflower* at the very end of the book (if you are not using *A Seed in Need*, you can use another labelled diagram of a plant or flower).
● Ask the children to think about why there are lines from the flower to some interesting writing.
● Read the labelling and establish that the lines are joining written information to the relevant part of the plant.
● Discuss how pictures and diagrams can help to put information across to the reader more easily.
● Organise the children into groups of about four and give them two or three information books.
● Ask them to look for other diagrams or pictures that have similar labelling.
● Share some of the children's findings to reinforce their understanding of diagrams and labels.
● Now that the children have explored the way pictures and diagrams work, suggest providing a page in their class book that provides information in a similar way.
● Prepare a table with items you will need to plant seeds: a plant pot (use a plastic pot from a garden centre), a plant pot saucer (use a round margarine carton lid), compost contained in a margarine tub, seeds in a bottle top, a watering can with a small amount of water and a sticky label to put on the pot.
● Involve the children in writing labels on cards and using string to join them to the items to make a 3-D diagram.
● Use the words the children offer for the labels to expand orally on the reasons for some of the improvised equipment. For example, *the margarine lid acts as a saucer*.

Guided work

● Work with two groups with a selection of non-fiction books to compare labelled diagrams and pictures.
● Read together the information contained in the labels and discuss the usefulness of the information and how it is laid out.
● Discuss why it would be difficult to put the information across without the picture.

Independent work

● Organise the children into pairs so that they can collaborate in creating a labelled picture of the things they will need for planting seeds.

Plenary

● Show the new page in the class book, encouraging the children to read the labels.
● Choose children to use a pointer to show that they can locate the correct label for the appropriate part of the diagram.

Planting seeds

Objectives

NLS

T25: To assemble information from own experience; to use simple sentences to describe.

S5: To continue demarcating sentences in writing, ending a sentence with a full stop.

S7: To use capital letters for the start of a sentence.

S&L

6 Listening: To listen and follow instructions accurately, asking for help and clarification if necessary.

What you need

● Seed-planting equipment and materials
● Polaroid or digital camera

Guided and independent work

● The guided session is at the beginning of this Hour, followed by shared work. Before the lesson, prepare tables with sufficient resources for pairs of children to plant seeds.
● Provide some adult support so that the children can engage in conversation that leads them into deeper thinking. For example, *How deep should we plant the seeds, will it make a difference?* The adult support should offer advice where required, for example in reading information from the back of the seed packets.
● Let the children take turns to accompany you in taking photographs of the process.

Shared text-level work

● After the practical activity is finished, gather the children around the board where you have randomly attached the photographs taken in the session (if possible, enlarge photographs to A4).
● Invite the children to talk about what is happening in the photographs and work together to arrange the photographs in chronological order to show the process.
● Once the order is agreed, fix the photographs on separate pages in the class book. This will require a separate page for each photograph; the number of pages will depend on the number of 'steps' the children have devised.

Shared sentence-level work

● Use this time for shared writing based on the question and answer model of the ladybird and the snail in *A Seed in Need*.
● Turn to the first photograph in the class book and encourage the children to pose a question about the picture, for example *Why is Paul putting compost in the plant pot?*
● Model the process of writing the question in the book to accompany the photograph, involving the children in decisions about capital letters and, in this case, a question mark. Pose questions about spelling the words accurately. However, because of time constraints, focus mainly on the content and act as scribe.
● Ask the children what could be said in response to the question, for example *Paul is putting compost in the plant pot so that the seeds can take root and grow.* Write the answer again directly into the book.
● It might not be possible to complete the whole book in this session, but completing the book would provide further useful opportunities for shared writing.
● Consider linking the project to art to provide drawings of narrators for the book and a colourful front cover.

Differentiation

● As a whole class activity, this will self-differentiate.

Plenary

● Conclude the session by reading together and enjoying the class book.
● Leave the book on display for reference in other lessons.

UNIT 3

Poetry

The following five hours concentrate on the enjoyment of listening to poetry. Children are encouraged through the shared sessions to make their own interpretations of the poems for deeper understanding and enjoyment. Through exploration of the texts and playing with words, children are led into composing their own lines of poetry. The unit is based on two poems: 'Chinese New Year' by Neela Mann (provided on photocopiable page 112) and *One Smiling Grandma: A Caribbean Counting Book* by Anne Marie Linden (Mammoth). Hour 3 covers similar work to *Progression in Phonics* Steps 4 and 5.

Hour	Shared text-level work	Shared word-/ sentence-level work	Guided work	Independent work	Plenary
1 Hear and see the poem	Reciting 'Chinese New Year'; discussing the meaning of the poem.	Creating -*ing* words.	Guided reading and discussion to further interpret the poem.	Interpreting the poem by drawing imagined pictures.	Discussing children's interpretations.
2 Learning by heart	Using actions to aid memory for learning to recite poem.	Creating alternative rhyming lines for the poem.	Guided reading and discussion to further interpret the poem.	Working together using actions to help them learn and practise the poem.	Performing the poem.
3 Being a poet	Inventing new poems about the Chinese New Year.	Creating new words by altering the vowel phoneme.	Using a word maker to compose new poems.	Using word maker, objects and discussion to compose group poem.	Sharing poems with children from different groups.
4 Poetry with a smile	Reading the poem with a focus on reading with expression.	Suggesting words that rhyme.	Reading for further interpretation and prediction.	Learning and reciting small sections of the poem.	Group reading aloud of the poem with expression and intonation.
5 Favourite lines	Re-reading and discussing to aid comprehension; composing additional lines.		Composing poems as in the shared session.	Composing poems as in the shared session.	Reading each other's lines aloud; compiling a class book.

Key assessment opportunities
● Can the children recite simple poems and read aloud with expression?
● Can they substitute and extend patterns from poems?
● Have they learned new rhyming words?

Hear and see the poem

Objectives

NLS
T11: To learn and recite simple poems and rhymes, and to re-read them from the text.
T13: To substitute and extend patterns from reading through language play, e.g. using same lines and introducing new words.
W7: To recognise the critical features of words, e.g. common spelling patterns.

What you need
● Photocopiable page 112.

Shared text-level work
● Recite the poem to the children. (Your knowing the poem by heart will encourage the children to learn it by heart too.)
● Let the children glean for themselves what the poem is about. Ask what it made them think of.
● To elicit further thoughts, tell the children to close their eyes and concentrate on the poem as you recite it again. Then ask what they were reminded of. What sounds and words made pictures pop into their minds?
● Focus on establishing the setting by inviting the children to explain their imagined pictures. Ask the children what words and phrases are associated with China and the New Year. For example: *What tells you there is a celebration? How are people celebrating? What words or phrases make you think that this celebration is from China? What words and phrases make you think that it is New Year?*
● Appreciate the full scene and let the children raise their own questions. Then confirm the celebration is for Chinese New Year.
● Recite the poem again, encouraging the children to join in.

Shared word-level work
● Display an enlarged version of the poem and read it together.
● Read it again, but this time focus on the words *bobbing* and *swirling*. Invite the children to explain what has been added to the words *bob* and *swirl* to make them rhyme.
● Ask the children for alternatives to *bob* and *swirl* to provide different rhyming lines, for example *pretty lanterns sway, sway, swaying; pretty lanterns turn, turn, turning*. Accept the children's suggestions even if they are pure invention, for example *pip, pip, pipping; dob, dob, dobbing*. Do the same for the next line *Lion dancers, whirl, twirl, swirling*.
● Explain that playing with words like this is what poets often do when they write poetry.

Guided work
● Re-read the poem with a group, reinforcing the children's understanding through guided discussion and supportive questioning.
● Encourage the children to try to predict words from memory.

Independent work
● Provide pairs with an A3 copy of the poem and ask them to illustrate it with the pictures that the poem conjures in their imagination.
● Encourage the children to discuss with each other what pictures they want to include and why, and where they want to put them.

Differentiation

Less able
● Support pairs' discussion of the poem.

More able
● Encourage the children to record and play back their discussion.

Plenary
● Choose two pairs to talk about the pictures they have included and why they chose them.
● Extend these explanations to clarify and deepen their own and others' interpretation of the poem.

UNIT 3 HOUR 2 ⬛ Poetry

Learning by heart

Objectives

NLS

T11: To learn and recite simple poems, with actions.

T13: To substitute and extend patterns from reading through language play, e.g. using same lines and introducing new words.

W7: To recognise the critical features of words, e.g. common spelling patterns.

What you need
● Photocopiable page 112
● craft materials.

Differentiation

Less able
● Help the children to make props that support the recitation, such as card fireworks, paper Chinese lanterns, lion masks, silk streamers for bodies to *twirl* and *swirl* and brightly painted dowelling for chopsticks.

More able
● Organise the children into pairs where one is responsible for learning and reciting the first and last line of each verse, whilst the other child is responsible for learning and reciting the two middle lines. The two children should work together to produce a collaborate recitation.

Shared text-level work
● Create a special performance area, perhaps by stringing lanterns around one edge.
● Display 'Chinese New Year' and recite it. Choose children to point to the rhyming words.
● Invite children to recite a phrase or two from memory. Encourage them to identify the bit of the poem they have remembered by pointing to the words in the text.
● Now devise actions for the poem. Organise a space for the children so that they have their own room to dramatise the actions. Begin by involving the children by inventing their own actions for the *fizzle, fizzle, BANG* of the firework. Similarly dramatise each of the three action lines in both verses. For the last line of each verse organise the children into pairs in order for them to dramatise wishing each other the sentiments of the line *Good luck, good health, good wealth.*
● Tell the children they will be developing this drama work in the group activities.

Shared word-level work
● Remind the children of their alternative rhyming lines from the previous session by referring to the collection you have on the flipchart.
● Display the poem and concentrate on the opening line from each verse. Ask the children what they notice about the sounds *BANG* and *CLANG.* Once they have established that the words rhyme, explore how both words sound loud, for example the ringing sound of *-ang* and the explosive sound of *b-.*
● Ask the children to provide alternative loud words for the explosive ending of each line. Further examine the lines to identify the rhyming words *fizzle* and *sizzle.* Draw the children's attention to the two-syllable structure of *fizzle* and *sizzle* as opposed to the one syllable structure of *BANG* and *CLANG.*
● Remind the children that they are exploring and playing with words to become poets.

Guided work
● Continue as Hour 1 with a different group.

Independent work
● Organise six areas in the classroom where groups of about five can work together to learn the poem and practise reciting it with appropriate actions. Explain that they will be performing the poem to the other children in the plenary.

Plenary
● Ensure the children appreciate the importance of being an audience by providing chairs to sit on in the performance area.
● Organise for each group in turn to perform the poem and encourage the audience to show their appreciation by applauding.

Being a poet

Objectives

NLS
T13: To substitute and extend patterns from reading through language play, e.g. by using same lines and introducing new words.
W1: To secure identification, spelling and reading of initial, final and medial letter sounds in simple words. **W10:** To learn new words from reading and shared experiences and to make collections of personal interest words and words linked to particular topics.

S&L
7 Group discussion and interaction: To take turns to speak, listen to others' suggestions and talk about what they are going to do.

What you need
● Word collections made in Hours 1 and 2
● photocopiable pages 112 and 113
● photographs, paintings and objects such as Chinese New Year carnival, lion and dragon dancers, all objects from the previous session.

Differentiation

Less able
● Encourage the children to use the word makers and generate ideas, but scribe for them if necessary.

More able
● Children in this group should endeavour to create more than one poem.

Shared text- and word-level work
● Praise the children for their poetic creativity by referring to the collections of new rhyming lines and words they have generated.
● Explain that together you are going to use some of their lines to invent new poems about Chinese New Year.
● Choose children to make selections from the collections on the flipcharts to compose a new verse. Encourage the children to talk about the pictures in the mind that the new verse conjures up. Then involve the children in providing other substitute lines based on the same patterns as the previous sessions.
● Ask the children if they would like to move the lines around to make the poems sound better or different, for example by changing the position of a loud sounding word from the beginning of the verse to the end of the verse, for example:

> Pretty lanterns, turn, turn, turning
> Lion dancers, curl, curl, curling
> Fireworks, crackle, crackle, CRACK

Shared word-level work
● To help the children create new words play at altering the vowel phoneme in words such as *bang* and *clang, bob, click* and *yum*.
● Further demonstrate this by using an enlarged blank word maker writing on your own and the children's suggestions.

Guided work
● Give each pair of children a word maker from photocopiable page 113 and have fun using it to make new words to try out for their collaborative poem.
● Help them to write their own poems now that they have lots of ideas and words to use.

Independent work
● Organise the classroom into four poetry writing areas. In each area prepare a table containing a selection of photographs and artefacts including those made by the children in Hour 2 for them to refer to and use as inspiration.
● Using the objects, word makers, and collaborative work so far, ask each group to work together to create a group poem on the topic of their area. Remind them to take turns to share ideas and organise themselves.

Plenary
● Organise the children to move around the tables in order to enjoy each group's poems.
● Provide opportunities for the children to share their poems with children from other classes.

Poetry with a smile

Objectives

NLS

T11: To learn and recite simple poems, and to re-read them from the text.
S1: To expect reading to make sense, and to read aloud using expression appropriate to the grammar of the text.
W7: To recognise the critical features of words, e.g. length, common spelling patterns.

S&L

9 Speaking: To interpret a text by reading aloud with some variety in pace and emphasis.

What you need

● The book *One Smiling Grandma: A Caribbean Counting Book*
● couplets from the poem written on cards
● tapes of you reading the poem.

Shared text- and sentence-level work

● Read *One Smiling Grandma* with the children, using lots of expression and enjoyment. Linger over the words and pictures to allow the children to interpret the emotions associated with each line.
● Re-read the first two lines together as you point to the words.
● Then choose children to read the next lines with appropriate expression, volume and pace. Read with the children so that they don't struggle with the words. The emphasis should be on reading with expression rather than struggling with decoding.

Shared word-level work

● Focus on rhyming words. Ask volunteers to point to two words that rhyme: *chair/hair, air/wares, sweet/beat, beach/reach, round/sound.*
● Use one of each pair as column headings on a large sheet of paper and invite children to suggest other rhyming words:

chair	sweet	beach	round
hair	beat	reach	sound
air	heat	peach	hound
stair	treat	leech	ground

● Keep the chart on display so that the children can add new rhyming words.

Guided work

● As you read the book together, reinforce the children's understanding through guided discussion and supportive questioning.
● Encourage the children to predict words, drawing on memory, the use of rhyme and the sense/context of the phrases.

Independent work

● Organise pairs of children in five groups where each group is designated a rhyming couplet from the poem.
● Tell the pairs to practise reading the rhyming lines to one another as they did in the shared part of the session.
● To support this activity provide some groups with the book so that they can refer to the pictures to help them recall the words and the sentiments. Also provide tapes of you reading/reciting the poem, so that they can hear the words written on their cards.

Differentiation

Less able
● Establish a listening centre (tape player and headphones) for the children to listen to the poem as they look at the book.

More able
● Ask the children to record and play back their reciting of the lines in order to discuss improvements.

Plenary

● Reinforce what you mean by being expressive by providing exaggerated examples, such as *smi i i i i i ling* so that saying the word causes you to smile. *Gliding* can be exaggerated in the same way.
● Ask individual children to pick out words or phrases that they like saying and hearing and demonstrate how to say them with the appropriate expression.
● Organise a class reading: choose a pair from each of the five groups to read their part of the poem one after the other.

Favourite lines

Objectives

NLS
T2: To use phonological, contextual, grammatical and graphic knowledge to make sense of what they read.
T12: Through shared and guided writing to apply phonological, graphic knowledge and sight vocabulary to spell words accurately.
13: To substitute and extend patterns from reading, e.g. by using same lines and introducing new words.

What you need
● The book *One Smiling Grandma*
● the table of words from Hour 4.

Shared text-level work
● Begin the session again by sharing *One Smiling Grandma* with the children.
● Ask the children to choose their favourite line and explain why it is their favourite.
● Use the children's suggestions to focus on alliterative patterns such as *birds sipping nectar sweet* and *five flying fish*.
● Encourage the children to make connections between what is happening in the poem and their own experiences. For example, visiting Grandma or her visiting them, Mother helping them to get ready for the day, wildlife they encounter near their home or school, bands or parades they have seen playing in the street or at the park, swimming in the sea on holiday.
● Make sure that the children can see the table of words from Hour 4 so that they can create new lines of poetry.
● Write on the board the first line from the poem, *One smiling grandma in a rocking chair.*
● Remind the children of their thoughts about their Grandmas earlier in the session and ask them if they can think of ideas to replace *in a rocking chair,* for example *making a cup of tea, knitting a scarf, walking a little dog*
● Check spellings and sounds and, if any of the suggested words rhyme with those in the chart, ask the child to add it to the correct column. Allow other children to help with spelling if necessary.
● Suggest to the children that by changing the word *Grandma* they could create a line about someone else.
● Ask for suggestions of another person to write about, for example *Mummy, Jennifer, Ravi, brother, grandpa* then go through the line, and allowing the children to make the decisions, change the lines appropriately.
● Leave this shared writing on display for reference in the rest of the session.

Guided work
● Work with a group to continue the composing process as in the shared writing, substituting words as and where the children decide.

Independent work
● Ask the children to write about Grandma in the same way that you demonstrated in the shared session.

Plenary
● Organise the children into pairs so that they can read their poems to each other. Then choose children to read aloud their partner's line(s) to the class.
● Collect the children's lines of poetry to make into a class book for them to read at other times. Illustrations could be included to complement their writing.

Differentiation

Less able
● Provide the children with the opening *One smiling grandma...* on a strip of card which they complete with classroom assistant support.

More able
● Encourage the children to substitute Grandma and write another line or verse.

Chinese New Year

Fireworks, fizzle, fizzle BANG

Pretty lanterns, bob, bob, bobbing

Lion dancers, whirl, twirl, swirling

Good luck, good health, good wealth.

Woks, sizzle, sizzle, CLANG

Dumplings, yum, yum, yummy

Chopsticks, click, clack, clicking

Good luck, good health, good wealth.

Neela Mann

Word maker

1. Cut out the strips, stick on to card and laminate.
2. Cut along the slits and thread the strips through from the back so that only one word will show at the front.
3. Move the strips to make new words.

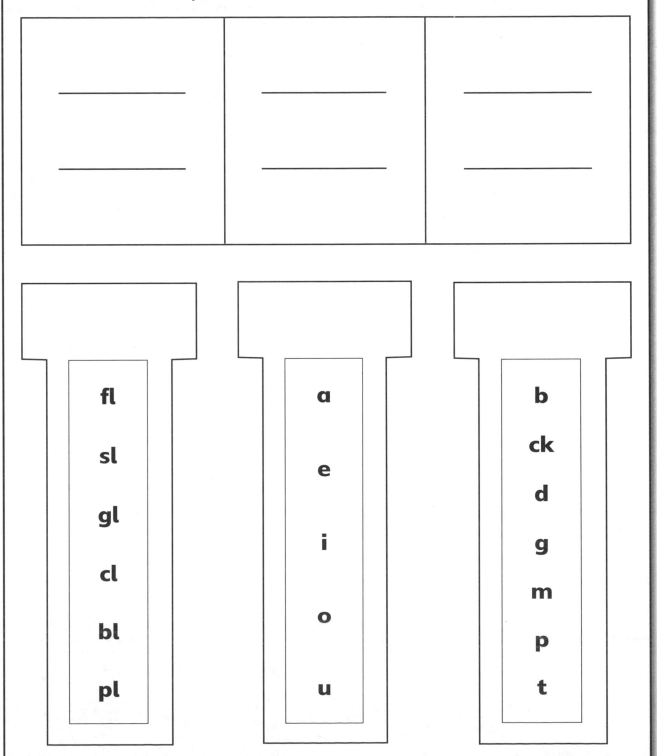

fl	a	b
sl	e	ck
gl	i	d
cl	o	g
bl		m
pl	u	p
		t

UNIT 4 🗋

Narrative 2

This first five hours of this unit are based on the story of 'The Imperial Nightingale', sometimes called 'The Enchanted Nightingale' or just 'The Nightingale'. It can be found in various collections of Hans Christian Andersen's stories and other children's anthologies. It is a story best told (rather than simply read), as Andersen himself would have done, leaving the teller to embellish and personalise the story. The nightingale's song can be found on a CD called *British Bird Sounds* from the British Library Collection. You could use a loop of this to enhance the storytelling and make links to non-fiction work. Singing, dancing and drama are the basis of the following five sessions on 'Sleeping Beauty', linking to PE and Unit 6 in *Developing Early Writing*. This drama work helps children's understanding of story sequence and develop identification of story figures' characteristics and ways of speaking. Hour 3 links to *Progression in Phonics* Step 5; Hour 9 links with 'Developing the concept of a sentence' in *Developing Early Writing*.

Hour	Shared text-level work	Shared word-/ sentence-level work	Guided work	Independent work	Plenary
1 Storytelling 💬	Listening to the story; discussing the opening.		Exploring a selection of fairy-story beginnings.	Comparing and collecting different story openings.	Sharing some of the story beginnings collected.
2 Story in pictures	Exploring the characters' behaviour and qualities to start telling the story.	Making a collection of bird names.	Sequencing story pictures; reading speech with expression.	Sequencing story pictures.	Telling the story through pictures and dialogue.
3 Character portraits	Exploring main characters.	Sorting bird names alphabetically.	Exploring characters by reference to the text.	Making character portraits.	Discussing characters in small groups.
4 Telling the story to each other	Consolidating knowledge of the story.	Reinforcing strategies for spelling.	Making stick character puppets to tell the story.	Making stick character puppets to tell the story.	Discussing storytelling skills and how they remembered the story.
5 Story endings	Discussing endings in familiar stories.	Reinforcing alphabetic order and spelling strategies.	Comparing and discussing similarities and differences in story endings.	Comparing and discussing similarities and differences in story endings.	Discussing similar and different endings and whether they would change the ending of 'The Imperial Nightingale'.

UNIT 4 💭

Hour	Shared text level work	Shared word/ sentence level work	Guided work	Independent work	Plenary
6 Story song 💭	Learning the story song of 'Sleeping Beauty'.	Focusing on words ending in *-ong*.	Reading the story song.	Group reading and re-enactment of story song.	Watching a performance of the song.
7 Sequencing the story	Shared reading matching word said to word read.	Focusing on words ending in *-ing*.	Re-reading, working to develop reading strategies.	Reading verses from the song and collaborating to put them in order.	Reinforcing reading strategies; establishing story sequence.
8 Learning the story song by heart	Reading, singing and dancing verses.	Reading and sorting words ending in *-ing* and *-ong*.	Highlighting *-ing* and *-ong* words in the text.	Playing a 'pairs' game using words ending in *-ing* and *-ong*.	Reinforcing rhyme and associated letter patterns.
9 Making a story tape 💭	Begin to make a class story tape.	Writing a sentence using capital letter and full stop correctly.	Writing sentences from the tape.	Devising an oral retelling of the story.	Sharing stories in groups.
10 Embellishing the story tape 💭	Adding dialogue to the story.	Writing a sentence using capital letter and full stop correctly.	Working in role to suggest what characters might say.	Working in role to suggest what characters might say.	Role-playing the conversations to show how it contributes to a fuller picture of the characters.

Key assessment opportunities
● Can the children retell stories orally and in writing, drawing on key features of story language to demonstrate understanding of character?
● Do they understand what can make a good beginning and ending?
● Can they sort words alphabetically?
● Can they punctuate sentences appropriately?

UNIT 4 HOUR 1 ☐ Narrative 2

Storytelling

Objectives

NLS
T5: To identify and record some key features of story language and practise using them, e.g. in oral retellings.
10: To identify and compare basic story elements, e.g. beginnings in different stories.

S&L
5 Speaking: To retell stories, ordering events using story language.

What you need
● nightingale bird song on CD or tape
● selection of fairy stories
● selection of other storybooks
● photocopiable pages 126–128.

Differentiation

Less able
● Provide pairs with photocopiable page 128 to use as a prompt to tell each other the story.

More able
● Provide pairs with photocopiable page 128 cut up and jumbled. Ask them to place the pictures in sequence to retell the story.

Shared text-level work
● This session does not include word- or sentence-level work in order to allow additional time for the telling the story of 'The Imperial Nightingale'.
● The story will take between 20 and 30 minutes to tell properly and it would be inappropriate to detract from the context by including additional word- or sentence-level work. The main objective is for the children to listen and appreciate the oral storytelling.
● At the end of the storytelling, the focus will be on how you began the story, so, before starting, be aware of the beginning you choose: *A long time ago*, *Once upon a time*, *In a far and distant land* and so on.
● Begin by playing the recording of the nightingale's song. Allow time for the children to fully appreciate the sounds then ask if they know what bird it is.
● Establish that the bird in the recording is a nightingale and then proceed to tell the story in your own words, using plenty of expression and enjoyment.
● Engage the children in a short discussion about how you began the story. Ask:

> ● Can you remember how I began the story?
> ● How did I tell you about where the story was set?
> ● How did I tell you about the time when the story occurred?
> ● How did I tell you who the story was going to be about?

● Then ask the children to provide their own ideas for beginning the story. Can they draw upon their knowledge of other stories to make a suggestion?
● Tell the children that over the coming week you are going to help them become storytellers just like you.

Guided work
● Provide a number of fairy stories to reinforce text objectives. Encourage the children to discuss story beginnings by making links among the stories and with others they have read.

Independent work
● Organise the children into groups of four (these can be two sets of talk partners) and provide them with a selection of storybooks, including some fairy tales, with different beginnings.
● Ask the children to compare and make a collection of different types of beginnings.

Plenary
● Share some of the story beginnings collected. Encourage the children to read the beginnings from the books in which they found them. Ask if some of the beginnings they have found would make a good beginning for 'The Imperial Nightingale', and why.

Story in pictures

Objectives

NLS

T8: To discuss characters, e.g. behaviour, qualities; to speculate about how they might behave.
T9: To become aware of character and dialogue, e.g. by role-playing parts when reading aloud.
W10: To learn new words from reading and shared experiences and to make collections of words linked to particular topics.

What you need
● Photocopiable pages 128 and 129
● sugar paper
● a flipchart.

Shared text-level work
● Remind the children about the story you told in Hour 1. Attach the first picture from photocopiable page 128 to the board.
● Choose a child to start the story. Encourage him or her to think about the selection of story openings from the previous session, such as *A long long time ago in a country far far away, Many years ago in a far off land.*
● Establish what the emperor is doing and display his line of speech from photocopiable page 129: *'Why have I never heard the nightingale?'.*
● Read it together, then choose a child to say the line as they think the emperor would say it.
● Ask questions about how the emperor might feel when all the world knows about the most splendid thing in his empire, yet he doesn't.
● Move on to the next picture and display the emperor's next line of speech: *'Bring the nightingale to me!'.* Once again, draw upon children's strategies for reading to establish what is being said and then how it is being said.
● Talk about how the pictures and speech are providing a means of telling the story.
● Tell the children that some of them will be using the pictures and speech to help them tell the whole story.

Shared word-level work
● Tell the children that they are going to make a collection of bird names. Use a flipchart so that you can display the collection later. Write *nightingale* and ask the children to suggest other birds that they have seen or know about.
● The main objective is to reinforce initial sounds to assist spelling and reading, for example *n* for *nightingale*, *r* for *robin*, *sp* for *sparrow*. For some words, such as *robin*, which is phonically regular, you will be able to engage the children in the whole spelling.
● Tell the children to keep their eyes peeled for spotting different birds that they can add to the list.

Independent work
● Organise the children into pairs. Provide each pair with a large sheet of sugar paper on which to match the story pictures to the speech sentences, and to paste them down in sequence.

Guided work
● Work with two groups to establish the story as in independent work.
● Encourage the children to read the speech with expression.

Plenary
● Use the large version of the story produced collaboratively to involve children in telling the story through the pictures and dialogue.
● Display the large version on the wall for the children to refer to at other times.

Differentiation

Less able
● Provide support so that this group can collaborate to make one large version of the story as for independent work.

More able
● Encourage the children to explore how the speech is being said.

UNIT 4 HOUR 3 Narrative 2

Character portraits

Objectives

NLS
T8: To identify and discuss characters, e.g. behaviour, qualities; to discuss how they are described in the text.
T20: To understand alphabetical organisation.
W3: To segment clusters into phonemes for spelling.

What you need
● Photocopiable pages 130- 131
● the children's work from Hour 2.

Shared text-level work
● In this session you are going to discuss the two main characters to establish the pomposity associated with the emperor and the humility associated with the nightingale. Use a flipchart sheet for each character with a similar layout to photocopiable pages 130 and 131.
● Ask the children what sort of character the emperor is and collect some of their ideas on the flipchart, for example *cross*, *bad tempered*, *not very clever*. Ask them what has made them think this. Was it something the emperor did, or said, or thought? Was it what others thought about him?
● Remind the children of the change that the emperor underwent at the end of the story. Ask them what he said that showed he had changed. Display the caption *'Dear nightingale, I am so sorry'* and read it together.
● Examine the character of the nightingale in the same way by asking questions about what the bird did, said and thought, or what others said about the bird.

Shared word-level work
● Display the collection of birds' names from Hour 2. Add any other birds' names the children have spotted to the collection.
● Involve the children in sorting the bird names into alphabetical order. Discuss any second/third letter combinations to resolve the order, such as *blackbird* and *blue tit*.
● To reinforce phoneme knowledge, write *robin* on the board and involve the children in segmenting it by sound, *r/o/b/i/n*.
● Emphasise that two letters can make one sound by segmenting *blackbird* where the *ck* and *ir* make one sound: *b/l/a/ck/b/ir/d*.

Guided work
● Reinforce text-level work by encouraging the children to discuss characters and support their descriptions by reference to the text.

Independent work
● Organise the children in pairs and allocate each pair either photocopiable page 130 or 131 to discuss and write about the character. Provide their work from Hour 2 as support.
● Ask the children to write what they think the character was like underneath the portrait, then explain why they think that by writing about what the character did, said and thought, and what others said or thought.

Differentiation

Less able
● Let the children draw the character of their choice. Encourage them to provide a description and refer to action, speech or thought.

More able
● Ask the children to concentrate on what others said or thought about the emperor.

Plenary
● Organise the children into groups of four so that in each group there are children who can talk about the nightingale and the emperor. Ask them to share their ideas about the characters.
● Reinforce the children's understanding of how what a character does and says and thinks contribute to our understanding of the character.

Telling the story to each other

Objectives

NLS
T4: To re-tell stories, giving the main points in sequence and to notice differences between written and spoken forms in re-telling.
W3: To blend phonemes in words with clusters for reading.

What you need
● Photocopiable pages 129, 132 and 133
● lollipop sticks, straws or dowels.

Shared text-level work
● The children will have gained a sense of the story and the characters through the work in the previous three sessions.
● Remind the children of the overall objective for them to become storytellers 'just like you'.
● This session reinforces the children's knowledge and understanding of the story and its sequence.
● Display an enlarged version of photocopiable page 129. Work through each statement, identifying who says it and encouraging the children to say the words as they think the character would say them.
● Ask each speaker to tell the class what is happening at that point in the story.
● Conclude this part of the session by praising the children for knowing the story so well and explaining that they will be telling the story to one another later in the lesson.

Shared word-level work
● Attach an enlarged picture of one of the birds from photocopiable page 132 to the board, along with the bird names from the bottom of the sheet.
● Choose a child to read and match the correct name to the bird. Encourage the child to talk about the reading strategies that he or she is using. Ask:

> ● Did you recognise the first letter?
> ● Can you blend any of the letters together to help read the word?
> ● Were there any other parts of the word that helped you know what it was?
> ● Was there a word inside the word that you already knew, for example 'black' in 'blackbird', 'sea' in 'seagull'?

● Do this for two or three bird pictures. Ask the children to help you add any new bird names to the class collection. As an additional task, the children could use photocopiable page 132 to match the pictures of the birds to the labels.

Differentiation

Less able
● Provide support to encourage discussion between the pairs and story prompts where necessary.

More able
● Organise the children into groups of three where two are the audience and one tells the story. Others should take turns to be storytellers if time allows.

Guided and independent work
● Organise the children to sit with their talk partners. Provide characters from photocopiable page 133 for the children to cut out, colour and decorate and attach to lollipop sticks or straws to use to tell the story to one another.

Plenary
● Discuss the children's storytelling skills. Ask them what helped them to remember the story. *What parts of the story were easy to remember and why? Were parts that were difficult to retell? Why?*
● Choose one or two children to retell specific parts.

Story endings

Objective

NLS

T10: To identify and compare basic story elements, e.g. endings.

What you need

● Big Books of familiar fairy stories or the endings written on flipchart paper
● photocopiable page 130.

Shared text-level work

● Tell the children that the endings of stories are as important as the beginnings, and involve them in a brief discussion about the ending of 'The Imperial Nightingale'.
● Suggest a different story ending such as the mechanical nightingale being repaired. Ask the children how they would have felt if this had been the case.
● Refer to other fairy stories to explore endings further, for example 'The Three Little Pigs', 'The Three Billy Goats Gruff', 'Little Red Riding Hood' and 'Cinderella'. Briefly recap the stories and read the endings. Pick out similarities and differences.
● Then tell the children an 'incorrect' ending of a fairy story, for example, for 'Goldilocks and the Three Bears': *The bears were so pleased to see Goldilocks sleeping in Mummy Bear's bed that they pulled the covers up and kissed her goodnight.* The children will probably be desperate to give you the correct version!
● Ask questions that encourage the children to think about the reasons for particular endings. Perhaps: *Served the wolf/troll right; So they would live happily ever after.*
● Refer to 'The Imperial Nightingale' and establish the reasons for its ending. Ask: *Why do you think the nightingale came back? Why do you think the emperor recovered when he heard the nightingale?*
● Conclude this part of the session by asking the children how they like to feel at the end of a story. Did they feel good at the end of 'The Imperial Nightingale'? Why?

Shared word-level work

● Repeat the activity from Hour 4, then sort the collection alphabetically.
● The collection of bird names could be used as a starting point for children's own stories.

Guided work

● Provide a number of fairy stories and ask the children to compare and discuss similarities and differences in the endings.

Independent work

● Organise the children into groups of four (these can be two groups of talk partners) and provide a selection of familiar fairy stories and traditional stories for children to make comparisons of the endings.
● Challenge the children to find two endings that are similar and two that are very different.

Plenary

● Choose children to talk about stories with similar endings and stories with very different endings.
● Now they have read lots of endings, ask the children if they would change anything in the ending of 'The Imperial Nightingale'.

Differentiation

Less able
● Give each pair a familiar picture book and support reading and discussion and comparison of its ending and the ending of 'The Imperial Nightingale'.

More able
● Encourage the children to make reference to story language, characters, whether the story is happy, sad, funny and so on.

Story song

Objectives

NLS
T11: To learn and recite simple poems and rhymes, with actions, and to re-read them from the text.
2: To investigate, read and spell words ending in *ng*.

S&L
8 Drama: To act out well-known stories, using different voices for characters.

What you need

● A role play corner with props, e.g. tiara, capes, boots, hobby-horse, cardboard sword, wand
● photocopiable pages 134 and 135.

Shared text-level work

● Display an enlarged copy of photocopiable page 134 on the classroom wall.
● Ask the children if they can tell you the story of 'Sleeping Beauty' in their own words. Then tell the children that they are going to learn the story through song and dance.
● Organise the children in a circle and, with the support of the classroom assistant, teach the children the story song of 'Sleeping Beauty'.
● Read the plain text first before combining with actions (see photocopiable page 134).
● Practise the rhythm and talk through difficult words like *dwelt*. Establish characters, events and setting.

Shared word-level work

● Focus on the word ending *ong* as in *long* and *song*. Write *song* on the board in large lower-case letters and choose a child to read the word.
● Ask another child to find the same word ending in the story (*long ago*).
● Tell the children that you want them to suggest other words that rhyme with *long* and *song* and remind them this is the 'story song' of Sleeping Beauty, emphasising the rhyme *song*.
● Make a collection of the children's words on a flipchart sheet, for example *gong* and 'sound words' such as *dong* and *bong*, involving them in the spellings.
● Display this word bank for reference during the unit.

Guided work

● Help the children to read the text on photocopiable page 134, encouraging the children to discuss the strategies that they are using to read new words.
● Focus on the important words and phrases that can be represented in actions, for example *big high tower, cast a spell, slept*.

Independent work

● Organise the children into groups of four to act out 'There was a princess long ago'.
● Give each group a copy of photocopiable 135 to use as a prompt as they go through the verses to construct the story.
● Tell them that to help them act out the story one person should be the princess, another the wicked witch, another the forest and another the prince.
● Encourage them to develop the actions they have practised in the story song.

Plenary

● Organise the children into an audience so that they can watch a performance from the children who have been using the role-play area.

Differentiation

Less able
● Encourage the children to use the props in the role-play area.

More able
● Before children begin to act out the song, support a discussion to explore characterisation so that children can embellish the song with expression and improvisation.

Sequencing the story

Objectives

NLS
T1: To reinforce and apply their word-level skills through shared and guided reading.
T4: To retell stories, giving the main points in sequence.
W2: To investigate, read and spell words ending in *ng*.

What you need
● Photocopiable page 134, including copies cut into verses
● envelopes for the verses
● large sheets of sugar paper.

Shared text-level work
● Display photocopiable page 134 and read the text carefully together.
● Use a pointer to point to each word being read, involving the children in pointing and reading.
● Reinforce reading strategies by choosing some children to explain what they are doing to read a new word.
● Encourage some other children to revise the actions to particular words as the children read them.

Shared word-level work
● Write the word *king* on the board, linking it to the royal people in the story, and choose a child to read the word.
● Tell the children that you want them to suggest other words that rhyme with *king* to make a collection as they did for *song* in the previous session. Words might include *sing, ding, ping, ting, wing, bring, string, thing*.
● If the children do suggest any verbs ending in -ing, remind them that words such as *ringing, singing, running* also rhyme with *king*.
● Involve the children in spelling the words. Ask them if they can see or hear any words sounding like *king* in the story song, for example *sleeping* and *riding*.
● Display this word list alongside the collection of *-ong* words.

Guided work
● Read photocopiable page 134 with the children, discussing the strategies they are using to read new words.
● Involve the children in explaining what they are doing to read a new word so that you can provide other appropriate strategies. For example, if a child is relying too heavily on one strategy, maybe phonics, encourage him or her to read on to make sense of what is being read.

Independent work
● Organise the children into groups of four as for Hour 6.
● Give each member of the group two of the verses of the story song. (One child will have three verses).
● Ask the children to take turns to read the verses then to work together to put them in the correct order.
● Suggest that they read them through again to check the whole story before pasting the strips on to a large sheet of sugar paper that can be illustrated in a painting or drawing session later.

Differentiation

Less able
● Help the children to put themselves in order as they sequence the sentences from the story.

More able
● Provide each pair with the verses of the story jumbled in an envelope with their names on. They can then sequence them and paste them on to sugar paper.

Plenary
● Reinforce reading strategies by choosing children to pick and read verses from their story song.
● Establish the sequence of the story by randomly handing out verses to the children, then asking them to stand up and read their verse at the appropriate time.

Learning the story song by heart

Objectives

NLS

T11: To learn and recite simple poems and rhymes, with actions, and to re-read them from the text.

W2: To investigate, read and spell words ending in *ng*.

W10: To learn new words from reading and to make a collections of words.

What you need

● Photocopiable page 134
● photocopiable page 136 copied on to card and cut up
● labelled cloth bags of *ong* and *ing* words on cards.

Shared text-level work

● Read the story song about the princess from photocopiable page 134 with the children.
● Then organise the children into nine groups, one for each verse of the song.
● Begin reading the story together again.
● After each verse, ask the appropriate group to act and sing their version of that verse. Encourage the children to use plenty of expression and enjoyment as they sing.
● Re-read or recite the complete song, asking each group to provide their verse, this time without the actions.

Shared word-level work

● Place the collections of *ong* and *ing* word cards face down, unread, on a table in a jumbled fashion.
● Choose children to select cards from the table, show the word to the class, read it and place it in the correct cloth bag.
● Draw the children's attention to the shared *ng* ending of words in both collections. Ask them what letter has changed to make the sounds *ong* and *ing*.
● Continue until all the bags have been used.

Guided work

● Read photocopiable page 134, asking the children to circle or highlight any words ending in *ng* as they read.

Independent work

● Organise the children into groups of four to play 'Pairs' from photocopiable page 136.
● You will need two copies of the photocopiable sheet and the sheets need to be cut up so that you have two copies of each word card.
● Ask the children to jumble both sets of cards and spread them out face down on their table.
● Explain to the children that the aim of the game is to find and win pairs of cards.
● Tell the children to take turns to turn over and read two cards. If the words match, they keep them, if not they turn them back over in the same place.
● Children should soon learn to memorise the position of cards in order to pick pairs!

Differentiation

Less able

● Support this group as they play the same game as in shared word-level work.

More able

● Give pairs some of the *-ing* and *-ong* word cards and encourage them to write rhyming words.

Plenary

● Ask the children from the higher ability group to share the words they have added to their own collections of *-ong* and *-ing* words.
● Reinforce strategies for reading the words and using the end sound of a word to suggest other words that rhyme.

UNIT 4 HOUR 9 ⬜ Narrative 2

Making a story tape

Objectives

NLS
T4: To retell stories and to notice differences between written and spoken forms.
S5: To continue demarcating sentences in writing, ending a sentence with a full stop.

S&L
5 Speaking: To retell stories, ordering events using story language.

What you need
● Tape recorders or dictaphones
● photocopiable page 134.

Shared text-level work
● Tell the children that in this session, with their help, you are going to record a version of 'There was a princess long ago'/'Sleeping Beauty' as a story-tape.
● Begin by asking the children for suggestions for the story's beginning.
● Record these on to tape and play them back. Discuss improvements in order to shape the beginning of the story and re-record parts where necessary.
● Continue by involving the children in telling the next part of the story.
● As this develops, draw comparisons between the text of the story song and the oral version being constructed on the tape recorder.
● Discuss the language the children are using to construct the story.
● Don't try to construct the whole story in the shared session; concentrate on identifying and recording some key features of story language. For example, discuss how the tone of the story changes when the wicked fairy is introduced.
● Encourage the children to use words that describe the wicked fairy's evil actions. Ask questions about the witch's motives such as *Why do you think the witch wanted to cast a spell over the princess?* so that children can think of issues such as jealousy and wickedness.
● Conclude this part of the session by telling the children that some of them will continue making the story-tape in group activities.

Shared sentence-level work
● Listen to the tape to see if there are any exciting sentences that you could use in shared writing – for example an opening sentence or a sentence that describes the princess.
● Focus on the use of a capital letter to begin the sentence and a full stop to end the sentence. Reinforce learning from Term 1 that a line of writing is not necessarily a sentence.

Guided work
● Work with small groups of children to take down sentences from the story-tape to demonstrate their construction in writing.

Independent work
● Organise the children to work in groups of four to construct a full oral retelling of 'Sleeping Beauty'.
● Advise them to be prepared to tell their story to another group in the plenary.

Plenary
● Organise for two groups to sit together and tell each other their story of 'Sleeping Beauty'.
● Include children from the more and less able groups to join in listening to the stories.

Differentiation

Less able
● Support this group in making a story-tape of just the beginning of 'Sleeping Beauty'.

More able
● Delegate the classroom assistant to help this group to complete a full, refined story on tape using the one begun in the shared work.

Embellishing the story tape

Objectives

NLS
T5: To identify and record some key features of story language, and to practise using them, e.g. in oral retellings.
T9: To become aware of character and dialogue, e.g. by role-playing parts.
S7: To use capital letters for the start of a sentence.

S&L
8 Drama: To act out well-known stories, using different voices for characters.

What you need
● Photocopiable pages 137 and 138
● additional copies of class story tape.

Shared text-level work
● Tell the children that you are going to play the story-tape from the previous session.
● Ask them to listen carefully and think of places in the story where they could make it sound better.
● Suggest that they might want to include what the characters say, that is, introduce dialogue.
● Ask the children, for example: *When the wicked fairy casts her spell, what do you think she might say to the princess?* (She might say, for example: *Now you will sleep forever!*)
● Reinforce children's understanding of character by choosing a child to *say* the words *Now you will sleep forever!* or your own chosen words in the way they think would be said by the wicked fairy – in a nasty, croaky, screechy, mean voice.
● Do the same for the part in the story when the prince sees the princess asleep. Ask: *What do you think he might say to the princess? How might he say it?*
● Suggest, for instance, that he would want to be quiet and soft, and perhaps a little hesitant, to wake her up gently.
● Conclude this part of the session by telling the children to use what more they have learned about the characters and what they say when re-enacting the story.
● Discuss with the children how the dialogue makes the story more interesting, realistic and lively.

Shared sentence-level work
● Use another sentence from the story-tape to play to the children to demonstrate how to construct a sentence in writing.
● As in Hour 9, reinforce the key sentence objectives of capital letter to begin a sentence and full stop to end.

Differentiation

Less able
● Allocate either photocopiable page 137 or 138 and encourage paired work.
● Organise for children to listen to the class story-tape and choose their favourite part of the story to tell to the classroom assistant.

More able
● Ask the children to use the role-play area to act out the story, using the story-tape as a 'script', together with their suggested dialogue embellishments.

Guided and independent work
● Organise the children to work in pairs. Give each pair photocopiable pages 137 and 138.
● Ask the children to establish what is happening in the pictures, then work in role to make up some lines of dialogue for each picture.
● Advise the children to practise a few ideas orally before beginning to write.
● Encourage them to use what they have learned about constructing and punctuating sentences.

Plenary
● Choose one or two pairs of children to present their conversation between the characters in the pictures. Remind them to speak in role.
● Reinforce the children's understanding of the way in which what is said by and to a character contributes to a fuller picture of that character.
● Make time to add these dialogues to the story tape.

The Imperial Nightingale (1)

In a splendid palace far, far away lived an emperor, surrounded by the most beautiful treasures. One day an envoy from another country arrived with the gift of a book about the emperor's country. It pleased the emperor to read about all the precious things he owned. But as he read on he was astonished to find that the book said that *the* most beautiful thing was the song of the nightingale.

"What is this?" said the emperor. "The nightingale? Why have I never heard the nightingale? Bring the nightingale to me!" he demanded.

His cavalier rushed around, but no one in the palace had heard of the nightingale. He went to the kitchens and cried out "Has anyone heard of the nightingale?"

The poorest little kitchen maid said, "Oh yes. I know where he lives. He sings to me so beautifully when I walk home through the woods."

"Little kitchen maid," said the cavalier. "Take me to the nightingale and you will be invited to hear him sing for the emperor."

So the cavalier and the courtiers followed the girl to the woods. At last they stopped, and they heard a beautiful song; it was the nightingale at the top of her favourite tree.

The cavalier and courtiers agreed it was the most delightful sound they had ever heard, but what a drab, small brown thing he was. The little girl thought otherwise, however; To her, the nightingale was as pretty as his song. She spoke to the bird, "Little nightingale, our gracious emperor wants you to sing just for him."

The nightingale replied, "I would be honoured to sing for the emperor, as I am honoured to sing for you."

The nightingale flew into the branches of the tall tree that grew outside the emperor's bedroom and he sang the most beautiful song to him. The emperor was deeply moved. Tears of joy rolled down his cheeks.

"Such a catchy tune. What can I give you as a reward for your singing to me?" the emperor asked the nightingale.

"Your tears are all I want as a reward," he replied graciously.

But then the emperor said that the nightingale must sing at his bidding. The nightingale said he would come

The Imperial Nightingale (2)

and sing each day, but this wasn't enough, so the nightingale was put in a golden cage.

When the little kitchen maid saw what had happened to her friend, she was upset that she had ever brought the bird to the palace.

Meanwhile, the emperor had received another gift. "What have we here?" he said, unwrapping it. He was delighted to find a jewelled mechanical bird. He wound the key in its side and it began to sing.

The emperor thought this mechanical bird was so beautiful, unlike the drab nightingale, that he would much prefer to have this one sing for him. His courtiers all agreed how beautiful it was and how well it sang. This made up the emperor's mind and he took hold of the real nightingale and threw her out of his window. "Don't come back!" he shouted.

The emperor listened to his new toy every day and night. Then, after a while, something terrible happened. In the middle of a song a bang and a clang and a rattle came from inside the bird, and then it burst apart. Wheels, springs, jewels and fake feathers flew everywhere. The emperor was distraught. "Fetch me my watchmaker!" he bellowed.

But the watchmaker couldn't mend it. "All the parts are worn out through over use."

The emperor was so sad that he fell ill. His doctors couldn't make him well again and they agreed that he was going to die.

When this news reached the kitchen, the little maid knew what she had to do, and she set off into the woods to find the nightingale.

"Dear nightingale, I am so sorry for the way you have been treated but can you find it in your heart to sing once more for the emperor? He will surely die if you don't."

"I will come again," he said and flew back to the tree outside the emperor's room and began to sing. When the emperor heard the song he began to smile and his cheeks began to colour. He regained his health and was happy, as was the little girl.

This time, the emperor made sure that the nightingale was free to come and go as she wished, and she came and sang for him each evening.
Based on the story by Hans Christian Andersen

TERM 2

Picture story

Who says what?

1. "Why have I never heard the nightingale?"	**2.** "Bring the nightingale to me."	**3.** "I know where the nightingale lives."
4. "Such a catchy tune."	**5.** "What can I give you as a reward for singing?"	**6.** "Your tears are all I want as a reward."
7. "What have we here?"	**8.** "Fetch me my watchmaker!"	**9.** "Don't come back!"
10. "I'll never mend this."	**11.** "Dear nightingale, I am so sorry."	**12.** "I will come again."

TERM 2

Portraits – the emperor

■ Write about this character.

What he said

What he thought

What he did

What others thought and said about him

The Emperor

Portraits – the nightingale

■ Write about this character.

What he said

What he thought

What he did

What others thought and said about him

The Nightingale

TERM 2

Spot the bird

sparrow	**blue tit**
blackbird	**pigeon**
thrush	**seagull**
robin	**magpie**

◣ SCHOLASTIC

Characters

There was a princess long ago

1. There was a princess long ago, long ago, long ago
There was a princess long ago, long long ago

2. And she dwelt in a big high tower, a big high tower, a big high tower
And she dwelt in a big high tower, long long ago

3. A wicked fairy cast a spell, cast a spell, cast a spell
A wicked fairy cast a spell, long long ago

4. The princess slept for a hundred years, a hundred years, a hundred years
The princess slept for a hundred years, long long ago

5. A great big forest grew around, grew around, grew around
A great big forest grew around, long long ago

6. A handsome prince came riding by, came riding by, came riding by
A handsome prince came riding by, long long ago

7. He chopped the trees down one by one, one by one, one by one
He chopped the trees down one by one, long long ago

8. He woke the princess with a kiss, with a kiss, with a kiss
He woke the princess with a kiss, long long ago

9. So everybody's happy now, happy now, happy now
So everybody's happy now, happy now.

Actions and music

1. Everyone makes a circle. Choose a child to be the princess in the middle of the circle.

2. Everyone joins hands to make the shape of a big high tower.

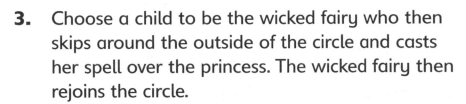

3. Choose a child to be the wicked fairy who then skips around the outside of the circle and casts her spell over the princess. The wicked fairy then rejoins the circle.

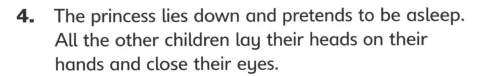

4. The princess lies down and pretends to be asleep. All the other children lay their heads on their hands and close their eyes.

5. Everyone pretends to be trees growing around the princess.

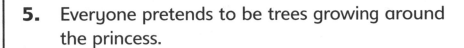

6. Choose a child to be the prince, who gallops around the outside of the circle.

7. As the prince pretends to chop down each tree the child responds by falling to the ground.

8. The prince enters the circle and takes the princess's hand, pretends to kiss it and she awakes.

9. Children in the circle together with the prince and princess raise and lower joined hands to show they are happy.

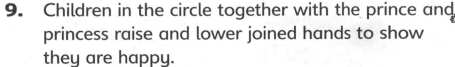

Pairs

king	ring	sing	ding
kong	song	dong	long
strong	prong	gong	pong
string	bring	spring	thing
swing	sting	wing	cling

SCHOLASTIC

What are they saying? (1)

TERM 2

What are they saying? (2)

UNIT 5

Non-fiction 2

The following five-hour unit links non-fiction work to science. While the context suggested is keeping caterpillars, the sessions could be adapted for any similar topic. Suggested reading is *Caterpillars* by Barrie Watts (Franklin Watts *Keeping Minibeasts* series), but the activities can be adapted for other non-fiction books and other topics. This unit ties in well with a science topic on minibeasts and their habitats. By the end of the unit, children should have worked in groups to set up their caterpillar habitats.

Hour	Shared text-level work	Shared word-/ sentence-level work	Guided work	Independent work	Plenary
1 Collecting questions and suggestions	Collecting suggestions for keeping caterpillars; navigating a non-fiction book.	Starting a collection of key topic words.	Demonstrating how to use a non-fiction book.	Researching the topic.	Evaluating the information found.
2 The dictionary	Introducing dictionaries.	Using alphabetical order to use dictionaries.	Finding topic words in a dictionary.	Finding topic words in a dictionary.	Explaining how to use a dictionary; reinforcing alphabetical order.
3 Indexes	Demonstrating how to use an index.	Looking at second letters to arrange words alphabetically.	Reinforcing work on indexes.	Using indexes to continue research.	Ordering words in an index.
4 A report	Compiling a report of the topic; revising work on sentences.	Compiling a report of the topic; revising work on sentences.	Creating a collaborative report.	Writing a sentence related to a given topic word.	Using children's sentences to create a logically sequenced report.
5 Contents page	Collecting ideas for a contents page in tjhe class book; using a contents page.	Focusing on plurals ending in *s*.	Collecting and writing ideas for the contents page in their class book.	Collecting and writing ideas for the contents page in their class book.	Constructing the contents page for the class book.

Key assessment opportunities
● Can the children read and navigate non-fiction texts?
● Can they use dictionaries, indexes and contents?
● Can they report on what they have done?
● Have they learned new topic words?

Collecting questions and suggestions

Objectives

NLS

T18: To read non-fiction books and understand that the reader doesn't need to go from start to finish but selects according to what is needed.

W10: To learn new words from reading and to make collections of words linked to particular topics.

What you need

● *Caterpillars* by Barrie Watts or appropriate non-fiction text (a Big Book is ideal)
● other information books on caterpillars and butterflies (for example, *Caterpillars and butterflies* by Stephanie Turnbull, Usborne)
● coloured paper 'bookmarks' on sticky notes.

Differentiation

Less able
● Organise the children to work as a group with the classroom assistant, examining non-fiction books, reading headings and looking at pictures.

More able
● Challenge the children with the additional task of collecting useful words for the class collection of topic words.

Shared-text level work

● Tell the children that they are going to keep caterpillars in the classroom to see how they grow and turn into butterflies. Explain that they are going to use information books to prepare for this.
● First, ask what sort of things they will need to know and collect their questions on the board. For example, *What will we feed them on? Will they need a special home? Do they need to be kept warm? Should we keep them in a light place or a dark place?*
● Introduce the book to show the children how to use a non-fiction text to answer some of their questions.
● Demonstrate glancing through the pages to spot headings and pictures that appear useful. Emphasise that there is no need to start at the beginning as with story books – information can be selected as needed.
● Choose children to come to the front to use the book as you did, asking them to explain why they have chosen a particular page.

Shared word-level work

● Tell the children that it would be useful to begin a collection of words for the topic. Ask them to suggest useful words they have used in the first part of the session and collect them on the board, for example *caterpillar, net, butterfly, windowsill, cage, nettles, jar, lid, air holes.*
● Display the list where children can add to it following their independent tasks.

Guided work

● Demonstrate further how to use a non-fiction book. Scan the contents and page headings, identify useful subheadings and pick out information about preparing to keep caterpillars.

Independent work

● Organise the children into groups of four and provide each group with a selection of books about caterpillars and butterflies.
● Tell the children to use the books as you did in the shared session, to see if they can find information they need to know for keeping and caring for caterpillars.
● Give the children strips of coloured paper or sticky notes for bookmarks so that they can refer to interesting pages in the plenary.

Plenary

● Share some of the information found. Select individual children to evaluate if the information they now have is sufficient for them to go ahead with keeping caterpillars.
● Link to science by establishing 'appropriate' housing for keeping caterpillars. Go on a caterpillar hunt, visit a butterfly farm or arrange for caterpillars to arrive by post!

The dictionary

Objectives

NLS
T20: To use simple dictionaries, and to understand their alphabetical organisation.

What you need
● Dictionaries
● topic word cards.

Shared-text level work
● Begin by showing the children a simple dictionary and ask them what sort of book it is. Ask:

> ● How do you think you might use this book?
> ● Do you know what a book like this is called?
> ● How do you know it isn't a story book?

● Reinforce the concept that dictionaries are used to find out what a word means or to check the spelling.
● Suggest a word associated with the current topic (check first that it is included in the chosen dictionary) and demonstrate how to find the word.
● Slowly talk through the process, emphasising how the alphabetical arrangement of the words helps you to find the chosen word.
● Repeat the process for a different word.

Shared-word level work
● Refer to the collection of topic words from Hour 1. Choose one of the words, such as *caterpillar*, and ask the children where they would find it in the dictionary – the beginning, middle or end? Select children to explain the reasoning behind their answers, making clear the link between the order of the words in the dictionary and alphabetical order.
● Write four of the topic words on large cards, ensuring there is good coverage of the alphabet, for example *nettle, caterpillar, butterfly, windowsill*, and give one to each of four children.
● Ask them to organise themselves into alphabetical order as they hold up their cards. To help them, ask which word would come first in the dictionary. Which would come last? So, which ones would be in the middle?

Guided work
● Reinforce how to use a dictionary with small groups of children, challenging them to find topic words and encouraging them to suggest their own to look up.

Independent work
● Organise the children into pairs and give each pair a simple dictionary. Also give them appropriate topic-word cards for them to find in the dictionary and read the information together. Encourage the pairs to challenge each other with spellings.

Plenary
● Ask one or two children to explain how to use a dictionary.
● Ask how the topic words were sorted into alphabetical order.
● Hold up a few cards again and ask the children to say which would come first, second, third and so on in a dictionary. Challenge the children to define or spell the words you hold up.

Differentiation

Less able
● Give the children simpler words to find.

More able
● Ask a group to work together to re-order the collection of topic words into alphabetical order. Challenge them to find as many as they can in the dictionary.

UNIT 5 HOUR 3 Non-fiction 2

Indexes

Objectives

NLS
T21: To understand the purposes of indexes and to locate information by page numbers and words by initial letter.
T1 W2: To practise and secure letter knowledge and alphabetic order.

What you need
● *Caterpillars* by Barrie Watts or other non-fiction book with an index.

Shared-text level work
● Remind the children how useful dictionaries are and how they are easy to use because of the way the words are ordered alphabetically.
● Tell them that alphabetical order is often used to help us find information elsewhere.
● Turn to the index page in the book and ask the children what they notice about the arrangement of the words. Then ask: *Why do you think there are numbers beside each word? What do the numbers tell you?*
● Select a child to use the book to choose a word from the index, find the page in the book and, with your support, read the information on the page, identifying the referenced word in the text.
● Do this several times to reinforce the procedure of using the word *index*.
● Involve the children in explaining what it means and understanding its function.

Shared-word level work
● Some of the children may already be aware of the need to consider second letters when placing words in alphabetical order.
● Choose three or four words from the topic words list that have the same initial letter but a different second letter, for example *caterpillar, container, chrysalis*.
● Write the words on the board in random order and ask the children how these can be sorted into alphabetical order when they all start with the same letter.
● Help them to establish the need to look at the second letter, then let them put them in the correct order.
● Repeat the activity with another set of words, such as *spins, sand* and *silk*.

Guided work
● Use your chosen non-fiction book and work with a group to reinforce how to use indexes.

Independent work
● Organise the children into groups of four. Give each group a collection of useful topic words, for example *containers, net, cage, foods*. Also provide each group with the book for locating the words in the index.
● Tell them to locate the appropriate pages and read the information by finding the index word in the text.
● This activity will also reinforce their knowledge and understanding about caterpillars.

Differentiation

Less able
● Help the children arrange the words into alphabetical order before using the index.

More able
● Tell the children to collect words from what they read that they might add to the index.

Plenary
● Involve the children who have collected additional words to find the correct alphabetical position for them in the index.
● Involve other children in the process and in a discussion about why they feel these words should be included.

UNIT 5 HOUR 4 ▭ Non-fiction 2

A report

Objectives

NLS
T25: To assemble information from own experience.
S2: To use awareness of the grammar of a sentence to decipher new or unfamiliar words.
S5: To continue demarcating sentences in writing, ending a sentence with a full stop.
W5: To read on sight other familiar words.

What you need

● Topic-word cards
● long strips of paper for writing sentences.

Shared text- and sentence-level work

● This session should take place after the children have set up the caterpillar 'farm' and begun caring for their caterpillars.
● Use this session to assemble their knowledge and understanding of the topic in order to write a simple report.
● Begin by asking what resources were needed to keep caterpillars and proceed to make a list, for example *jar, sand, nettles, net cage, lid, netting, foods.*
● Involve the children in recognising the words by handing the pointer to a child who then chooses and then points to a word for others to read.
● Then ask the children what steps they took. How did they set up their caterpillar homes? Encourage them to give detail in their answers.
● Proceed to order the list by asking the children what they needed to do first, what they did next, and so on. For example:

> *First* we needed a large jar with a lid.
> *Then* we made air holes in the lid.
> *Next* we made a cage and covered it with netting.

● As each sentence is constructed give the pointer to a child to point to words as they are read. Encourage the child to use appropriate reading strategies to read unfamiliar words such as using the grammar to predict reading on or reading back.
● Encourage the children to provide their own account, detailing their first-hand experience.
● Draw attention to the way in which the sentences are ordered, one piece of information linking to the next.
Use this opportunity to reinforce sentence structure by reminding the children that sentences begin with a capital letter and end with a full stop.

Guided work

● Work with a group to create a collaborative report of their experience of preparing to keep caterpillars.

Independent work

● Give each child a word card from the topic list (they don't all have to be different) and ask them to write a simple sentence or two of what they did related to the word, similar to what you did in the shared writing session.
● Provide long strips of paper to write on rather than large sheets, so that the children can bring them to the plenary for ordering into a non-chronological report.

Differentiation

Less able
● Encourage the children to tell you or the classroom assistant about what they did in relation to, for instance, *sand,* and scribe for them.

More able
● Expect the children to write more than one sentence.

Plenary

● Choose appropriate sentences to order into a report.
● Read the whole report through before displaying it in the classroom.

UNIT 5 HOUR 5 Non-fiction 2

Contents page

Objectives

NLS
T21: To understand the purpose of contents pages and to begin to locate information by page numbers.
W8: To investigate and learn spellings of words with s for plurals.

What you need

● *Caterpillars* or chosen book
● various non-fiction books with contents pages.

Shared-text level work

● Suggest that creating your own class information book about keeping caterpillars would be useful for the school library so that other children could use it when they want to keep caterpillars.
● Ask the children what information might be useful to include in their book. Collect ideas on the board in the form of general topics, for example *What you need to make a home for caterpillars, How to care for caterpillars, How to feed caterpillars, Watching caterpillars grow.*
● Then show them the contents page from the book. Show them that pages like this occur in lots of information books.
● Ask what the contents page is used for. Help the children to link their ideas on the board and the contents page.
● Remind them of how they used the index and explain that this page works in a similar way but is more useful for finding general information.
● Tell them that the numbers here refer to the *first page of a section* rather than individual entries. Point out that this list is in numerical rather than alphabetical order.
● Demonstrate how the contents page works and ask the children to help you by allowing them to:

> ● run their fingers along to the page number
> ● locate the page in the book
> ● read the heading
> ● match the heading to the contents
> ● see how many pages the section contains.

Shared word-level work

● Draw attention to the way in which you have been referring not to keeping *a* caterpillar or *one* caterpillar but rather *lots of caterpillars.*
● Ask the children what happens to the word when you talk about *one caterpillar* and *lots of caterpillars.* Demonstrate the singular and plural by writing the words on the board.
● Choose other appropriate words from the topic where adding *s* gives the plural: *lid, jar, nettle, container, cage* and so on.
● Be prepared to explain that not all words follow this pattern.

Guided and independent work

● Provide strips of paper for the children to write single ideas for the contents they would like to include in their class information book.
● Leave other contents pages on display as models.

Plenary

● Begin constructing a contents page in preparation for creating the class information book.
● Share and choose appropriate contents ideas and attach them to a large sheet of paper.
● Tell the children that as they continue to create their class book, they will be able to include the page numbers and order the contents page.

Differentiation

Less able
● Ask the children to work in pairs or small groups.

More able
● Once the children have written their entry, let them practise using the contents page in other books.

UNIT 1

Narrative 1

In this ten-hour unit, children rehearse stories through drama and role-play and focus on elements of story writing, incorporating these into their own stories. The writing is devoted to connecting incidents and inventing problems to solve. The unit links to the later unit on Poetry 2 (Term 3 Unit 4), and you may want to study the poetry unit first to spark the children's imaginations. Children use the role-play areas as starting points for acting out and telling stories of adventures in outer space. The children's imagined adventures will form many of the texts for literacy learning, but there are opportunities for the children to read some published fantasy world stories in story time, such as *The Trouble with Gran* by Babette Cole (Egmont), *Here Come the Aliens* by Colin McNaughton (Walker Books), *On the Way Home* by Jill Murphy (Macmillan) and *Q Pootle 5 in Space* by Nick Butterworth (Collins). The activities allow children to develop writing techniques to complete fantasy stories individually and collaboratively. By the end of the unit the children will have developed their understanding of story writing in an informed, stimulating and exciting way. Hours 3 and 10 link to *Progression in Phonics*, Step 7.

Hour	Shared text-level work	Shared word-/ sentence-level work	Guided work	Independent work	Plenary
1 Patrick's class topic	Establishing topic by reading a story.	Using grammar and punctuation to assist expression when reading aloud.	Focusing on strategies for reading.	Taking turns to listen to one another read and improve expression.	Evaluating story readings.
2 Naming the spaceship	Introducing role-play area for promoting imaginary stories.	Exploring spellings of labels associated with the topic.	Re-reading to highlight key topic words.	Writing spaceship nameplate and crew members' badges.	Naming the spaceship.
3 Settings for space stories	Using a- video of children in the role-play area to discuss story ideas and settings.	Exploring spelling patterns for the long vowel sound *i*.	Reading an outer space story to discuss settings.	Creating 3-D settings and characters for developing stories.	Telling one another about their ideas for stories.
4 Connecting incidents and events	Watching a video of children in the role-play area to identify and sequence story incidents.	Connecting events using common connective words.	Constructing a story orally.	Using their settings to develop story structure.	One group sharing their story; audience evaluating.
5 Developing the story	Linking events to form the beginning of a story.	Reinforcing sight recognition of high-frequency words used as connectives or in connective phrases.	Constructing story beginnings.	Writing the main elements of the plot, using their 3-D settings.	Sharing ideas; providing more useful connective phrases.

UNIT 1

Hour	Shared text-level work	Shared word-/ sentence-level work	Guided work	Independent work	Plenary
6 Problems everywhere	Comparing plots of familiar stories.	Reinforcing sentence construction in writing story problems.	Comparing stories (including their own).	Comparing stories (including their own).	Drawing conclusions about similarities and differences in stories.
7 We have a problem	Explaining the problems on board a spaceship, in role-play.	Constructing writing from speech.	Writing from a discussion of problems.	Suggesting solutions to the problem.	Reading each other's writing and suggesting how to improve.
8 More problems	Speculating what further problems might be happening.	Listing key words and phrases for fantasy world settings.	Working through problems and solutions.	Adding setting descriptions to stories.	Sharing settings and stories.
9 Writing a blurb	Using covers and blurbs to find out what stories might be about.	Writing a blurb in sentences.	Writing blurbs for their stories.	Writing blurbs that reveal the settings of their stories.	Saying what they have learned about blurbs.
10 💬 Literary critics	Annotating a text for preferences.	Sorting spelling patterns for long *i* vowel sound.	Discussing and explaining reasons for preferences in fantasy stories.	Discussing and explaining reasons for preferences in fantasy stories.	Identifying preferences; recapping learning over the unit.

Key assessment opportunities
● Can the children create fantasy world settings and use them to tell stories orally and in writing?
● Do they use connective words and phrases to join parts of sentences and sentences?
● Can they express and support their preferences?
● Do they listen with sustained concentration and speak with clarity and expression?

UNIT 1 HOUR 1 ▢ Narrative 1

Patrick's class topic

Objectives

NLS
T2: To use phonological, contextual, grammatical and graphic knowledge to work out, predict and check the meanings of unfamiliar words and to make sense of what they read.
S3: To read familiar texts aloud with pace and expression appropriate to the grammar e.g. pausing at full stops, raising voice for questions.

S&L
9 Speaking: To interpret a text by reading aloud with some variety in pace and emphasis.
10 Listening: To express views about how a story has been presented.

What you need
● Photocopiable pages 157 and 158
● reading prompt list (see Guided and independent work).

Shared text-level work
● Display photocopiable pages 157 and 158 and read the story aloud. Explain that the new class literacy topic is like the one in the story.
● Next refer to the text using a pointer to point to the words read. Ask children to use the pointer in the same way.
● Use this time to establish the meanings of any new words. Reinforce strategies for reading, especially predicting text from grammar, reading on, leaving a gap and re-reading.

Shared sentence-level work
● Re-read the first three paragraphs, up to *Keep up with the others please!*, but with no expression and at a flat pace. Establish what marks in the text indicate how it should be read, for example *speech marks, full stops, question marks, exclamation marks.* Ask the children to point out examples of these in the first three paragraphs.
● Involve the children in reading dialogue and questions In the opening text, establishing how the voice is raised slightly for asking questions and how full stops denote conclusions and so pauses in reading.

Guided work
● Work with two groups of children to read the whole story. Emphasise the strategies for reading as in the shared session.
● Once the children have established meanings, encourage them to practise reading aloud.

Independent work
● Organise the children to work in pairs to read the story together, using the punctuation to assist expression and pace.
● Then ask the children to take turns listening to one another and to make suggestions to improve reading.
● Place a 'what to do if I can't read a word' list on tables for children to refer to so that they can help one another. The list should include:

> Leave a gap, then re-read from the start of the sentence.
> Run on, see if the text makes sense and then re-read.
> Sound out a word or look for familiar patterns, then read to see if it makes sense.

Plenary
● Listen to children read one or two paragraphs and ask other children why they liked the readings. To draw attention to ways in which the children made their readings interesting, ask:

> ● Was the speech clear?
> ● Was it rushed?
> ● Was it good to speed up when he said...?
> ● Did slowing down...?
> ● Did you notice how he raised his voice?

Differentiation

Less able
● Emphasise using the grammar of sentences to aid understanding and interpretation.
● Make sure the children read the whole story once before trying to read aloud.

More able
● Ask the children to be specific and give demonstrations when helping one another to improve their readings.

UNIT 1 HOUR 2 ▢ Narrative 1

Naming the spaceship

Objectives

NLS
W5: To recognise words by common spelling patterns.
W8: To make collections of words linked to particular topics.
W10: To practise handwriting in conjunction with spelling and independent writing.

What you need
● Role-play areas: a spaceship and mission control
● video camera
● dictionaries
● photocopiable pages 157 and 158.

Shared text-level work
● Develop or set up the spaceship area from the poetry unit (see page 184) to include spacesuits and helmets; white overalls, a doctor's kit and science sample-collecting equipment; blue overalls, a safety helmet and tool kit for the engineer; a ship's log; a pilot's spacesuit with oxygen tanks. Also establish a further area for Mission Control.
● Remind the children of the story from the previous session where Patrick longed to go on adventures in space.
● Let small groups of children use the areas to explore adventures they might have on their way to distant planets.
● Bring the class together and discuss some of the children's ideas.

Shared word-level work
● Elaborate on the role-play areas by establishing the roles of various crew members, such as pilot, engineer, doctor, scientist.
● Talk about the need to provide labels like those on the children's coat pegs so that clothes and equipment can be kept in the right places.
● Note spelling patterns for the words needed. For example, examine the soft *sc* in *scientist* and use dictionaries to compare other words with similar beginnings: *scissors, scythe, scent* with the more common hard *sc* sound in *school, scab, scribble*.
● Establish the root word *engine* in *engineer*; the *or* sound pattern in *doctor* and similar words *tractor* and *motor*. Explore *pilot* with the long *i* sound.
● Explain that next they will need to think of a name for the spaceship, and at the end of the session, they will vote for their favourites. Suggest some well-known fictional and real spacecraft that might inspire their names, such as Starship Enterprise, Millennium Falcon, Challenger, Columbus, Apollo, Gemini, Eagle.

Guided work
● If additional support is available, ask the children to read 'Patrick's class topic' and highlight or list key topic words and phrases, such as *space, distant planets, outer space*.
● Look for common long vowel sounds, such as in *alien* and *space*.

Differentiation

Less able
● Give children scrap paper to practise their label writing before writing on cards.

More able
● Tell the children to use the role-play areas for inventing stories about journeys into outer space. Say that you are not going to interfere but film some of their play to watch in tomorrow's lesson.

Independent work
● Ask the children to work in pairs to write nameplates for the spaceship on large cards.
● Once they have a name, ask them to write smaller labels or badges for the crew members' uniforms.

Plenary
● Gather the children around the role-play areas. Collect names for the spaceship and vote for the favourite. Then name the spaceship in a ceremonial fashion: *I name this spaceship...* and attach the nameplate.
● Pin the chosen labels to the areas and display a list of all the suggested names.

Settings for space stories

Objectives
NLS
T14: To write stories using simple settings.
W1: To identify phonemes in speech and writing.

What you need
● A story book with an outer-space setting, such as *Q Pootle 5 in Space*
● video footage from Hour 2
● hoops and tabletop base boards
● small-world play resources
● craft materials
● 'Alien' poem from photocopiable page 191.

Shared text-level work
● Arrange to view the video from the previous session.
● Invite the children involved in the role-play to talk about and develop their ideas for stories and invite other children to contribute. Encourage them to use new vocabulary associated with the topic, for example:

- ● What special equipment do they need to explore the planet?
- ● What does the engineer/scientist/doctor/pilot have to do?
- ● Why do they need special clothes on the alien planet?

● Encourage all of the children to think about story settings and characters by asking:

- ● What might you see from the spaceship window?
- ● What do you imagine the planet you are travelling to will look like?
- ● What colours and textures might there be?
- ● Will there be strange plants and what do you imagine them to look like?
- ● Will there be humans on the planet or aliens like in the poem 'Alien'?
- ● Are there any buildings?

● Tell the children that they will be using the role-play area and making settings of outer space and planets to develop their stories.

Shared word-level work
● Remind the children of the long *i* vowel sound in *pilot*. Ask them to think of other words that have the same sound and collect them on the board, for example *sky, by, tie, night, rhyme, time, pie*.
● Work together to sort the words into columns based on spelling patterns and establish a chart for children to add to during the unit of work.
● Tell them that whenever they hear the sound in their reading or writing to write the word on the chart.

Differentiation

Less able
● Ask the group to use the role-play areas for inventing a story and tell them it will be their story you will be using to begin tomorrow's session. Record their exploration and discussion on video.

More able
● Ask pairs to use a cardboard box as the basis for creating a setting and characters with small world play resources.

Guided work
● Choose a story book with an outer-space setting for guided reading.
● Discuss the setting to encourage the children to invent their own settings when writing or role-playing.

Independent work
● Organise for the children to work in groups of four to create outer-space or spaceship settings and characters for their imagined stories. Useful props and materials might be: hoops and tabletop base boards, small-world play resources and figures, and craft materials.

Plenary
● Organise for representatives from the different groups to establish new groups to tell one another about the characters they have invented and the settings they have begun to make for creating stories

UNIT 1 HOUR 4 ■ Narrative 1

Connecting incidents and events

Objectives

NLS

T5: To retell stories, to give the main points in sequence and to pick out significant incidents.
T6: To prepare and retell stories orally, using some of the more formal features of story language.
W4: To read on sight more high-frequency words from Appendix List 1.

S&L

10 Listening: To listen to tapes or videos and express views about how a story has been presented.

What you need
● Video footage from Hour 3
● the children's settings from Hour 3
● cloth bag of connectives on cards, e.g. *so, suddenly, just then, after that, in a while, just when.*

Differentiation

Less able
● Allow the children to use the role-play areas to stimulate ideas. Provide enlarged connectives cards for children to refer to.

More able
● Ask the children to use their 'box' settings and develop more complex stories.

Shared text-level work
● View the video of the children's role-play from the previous session.
● Ask the children to discuss with their talk partners what they think the evolving story might be about.
● Assist the children to establish the story by inviting the children on the video to explain the roles they adopted, such as scientist, engineer, pilot, doctor.
● Focus on the events that were happening, beginning to happen or could happen and write these on the board, for example *We're going to crash! Let's explore the planet, We'd better run back to our spaceship.*
● Suggest to the children that they need to decide on the order of events now on the board and encourage the children to sequence them in order to establish a plot.

Shared word-level work
● Present the cloth bag of connective words and phrases. Reinforce the ability to read these on sight by choosing children to pull cards out of the bag and use them to link the imagined events on the board. For example:

> *Suddenly* we crash landed. *Just when* we thought it was safe to explore the planet we saw a weird alien *so* we ran back to the spaceship. *Just then* the pilot fainted. *Then* the engines failed *so* we sent for the engineer.

● Do this several times to string together a short series of events and so develop the plot of the fantasy story.

Guided work
● Work with a group to construct a collaborative oral fantasy story. Use the flashcards of connective phrases to support the rehearsal of the plot structure.

Independent work
● Organise the children into the same groups as in the previous session, with their settings. Tell them to use their settings to create or develop oral stories.

Plenary
● Choose one group to tell their story using their setting. Involve the audience in evaluating the story by asking:

> ● Can you tell me about the main things that happened?
> ● Where did the story take place?
> ● Who were the characters?
> ● What did you particularly enjoy?

Developing the story

Objectives

NLS
T14: To write stories using simple settings.
W3: To read on sight other familiar words.
W4: To read on sight more high-frequency words from Appendix List 1.

What you need
- Connectives flashcards from Hour 4
- photocopiable page 159.

Shared text-level work
- Use some of the children's settings and plot ideas to develop a story.
- Write down some of their suggestions for significant events, such as an engine failure in the spaceship or encountering an alien on a newly discovered planet.
- Demonstrate developing a written story by linking together two events that the children have suggested, drawing on the connective phrases used in the previous session. For example:

> Phoebe and Jaz were looking through the spaceship's window.
> Suddenly they felt the engines shudder.
> Phoebe and Jaz picked their way through the rocky surface. Just when they were about to turn back they heard a scary growl.

- Help the children to see the powerful words, such as *shudder* and *growl* and the more formal language of written stories.
- Demonstrate how by linking the events the beginning of the story is established to the point where the scene is set and the plot can begin to unfold with their further ideas. Emphasise to the children that a story must have a beginning, middle and end and what each of these sections should contain.

Shared word-level work
- Read the shared writing.
- To reinforce sight recognition, ask the children to point to familiar words and high-frequency words as you say them, for example *they*, *then*, *where*, *were*, *when*.
- Explore the spelling patterns of any new words, for example *shudder* and *growl*. Ask the children if they have seen these patterns in any other words.

Guided work
- Support groups in writing their individual stories by using their ideas developed orally in the previous session.
- Aim to establish the story to the point where the plot can begin to unfold towards its climax/conclusion.

Independent work
- Organise the children to work in the same groups as in previous sessions so that they can use their settings as a prompt for their individual story writing.
- Provide photocopiable page 159 so that they can write down the main elements of the story they have invented using the settings.

Plenary
- Arrange for the children to share each other's writing and story plots across the groups and discuss ways of developing their stories further.
- Add any new connective phrases to the collection in the cloth bag.

Differentiation

Less able
- Organise for the children to write in the role-play area so that they can act out scenarios before writing.

More able
- Encourage the children to write a whole short story. Provide connective phrases on cards to remind them how they can link two or three incidents together.

 151

Problems everywhere

Objectives

NLS

T8: To compare and contrast stories with a variety of settings.
S6: Through reading and writing, to reinforce knowledge of term *sentence* from previous terms.

What you need

● Collection of familiar stories, such as traditional tales, fairy tales and fantasy stories
● photocopiable page 160
● tape recorders.

Shared text-level work

● Tell the children that many stories are based around a problem, just like those they have been inventing in their stories.
● Show the children some well-known storybooks and ask them to identify the problems in the stories. For example:

> ● What is the problem Chicken Licken encounters? (The sky is falling down.)
> ● What is the main problem in 'The Three Little Pigs'? Is there more than one? (Wolf; houses not strong enough.)
> ● In 'Jack and the Beanstalk' there is a series of problems. What are they? (No money or food, the Giant and the Giant's wife, the talking harp.)

● Relate these to the problems in the children's space stories and draw out the similarities and differences.

Shared sentence-level work

● Ask the children to pose a problem related to their stories similar to Chicken Licken's problem when he thought the sky was falling down. Write Chicken Licken's problem and possible solution on the board and use it to write the children's invented problem:

> Chicken Licken had a problem. He thought the sky was falling down.
> So he went to see the King.
> The astronaut had a problem. He thought the spaceship was
> crashing. So he tried to reverse the ship using the rocket blasters.

Guided and independent work

● Organise the children into groups of four. Give each group a selection of familiar stories with a variety of settings (including their own stories) for them to compare and contrast through discussion. Ask them to focus on problems that arise in the story.
● Provide photocopiable page 160 and appoint one of the group to fill it in with the help of the other children. For example:

Book title	*The Trouble With Gran*
Author	*Babette Cole*
Setting	Familiar and then fantastic
Main characters	Gran and grandchild
What happens (include problem and how it is resolved)	Gran is secretly an alien who wants to do exciting things. She opens a travel agency so she can travel the world with her friends.
Illustrations	Start giving clues that Gran is an alien, like the antennae that grow larger through the story.

Differentiation

Less able
● Delegate the classroom assistant to support and prompt the children's discussion.

More able
● Ask groups to record their discussion on tape and play back so that they provide greater detail on the photocopiable sheet.

Plenary

● Draw some conclusions from what has been found, for example that problems occur in most stories, that imaginary places occur in lots of stories, that exciting things happen, that not all stories have animals.

We have a problem

Shared text-level work

● In role at Mission Control, tell the children in the form of an urgent news briefing that the spaceship orbiting planet Radon has developed a problem. It appears that the xenon converter has ruptured causing a serious drop in energy supply. The spaceship is spinning out of control, and if someone doesn't intervene, the consequences could be terrible.
● Tell the children that their questions and suggestions will be important for gaining control of the spaceship. Has anyone any ideas?
● Give the children some time, working in pairs, to discuss ideas before sharing them. Appoint the classroom assistant or a confident child (in role as science officer) to collect ideas using a tape recorder.
● Demonstrate the grave concern you have for this situation and your gratitude for all ideas.
● Play the tape and question the ideas to enable children to develop the suggested courses of action.

Shared sentence-level work

● Still in role, choose to adopt one of the suggestions from the tape. Share your thinking with the children so that they are part of the process of writing from speech.
1. First of all *listen* attentively to the taped suggestion.
2. *Repeat* it to the children so that everyone is clear about what they have heard.
3. *Write* the speech on the board. Ask the children if it sounds right and if they could make it sound better.
4. Then *redraft,* involving the children. This may involve taking out unnecessary and repeated words and punctuating the sentences. For example *He went to the engine room to mend the engine where an alien jumped on him. He shouted for help but no one could hear him.*

Guided work

● Establish problems that could arise in the children's individual stories through discussion. Then support the children in constructing writing as you did in the shared session and involve them in redrafting.

Independent work

● Organise the children to work in pairs so that they can collaborate in suggesting a solution for regaining control of the spaceship. Tell them to try out their suggestions orally before writing.
● They should then work together to write down the course of action, checking for composition and punctuation.
● The mini-story they create can be incorporated within their individual stories if appropriate.

Plenary

● Exchange pieces of writing between pairs so that they can read each other's work. Encourage positive feedback with suggestions for improving each other's writing.

UNIT 1 HOUR 8 ▪ Narrative 1

More problems

Objectives

NLS
T13: To write about significant events from known stories.
T14: To write stories using simple settings.
W8: To learn new words from reading and shared experiences.

What you need
● The children's fantasy world settings
● Mission Control commander costume (optional).

Shared text-level work
● This session builds on the previous one to reinforce understanding of problems and solutions that form the basis of many plot structures.
● Adopt the role of Mission Control commander again. Inform the children that the crew on the spaceship are working flat out to implement their suggestions, but other problems are arising. For security reasons, Mission Control has been asked not to reveal these to the public.
● Then, out of role, involve the children in speculating what the problems could be. Note some of these on the board.
● Choose a child from the higher ability group to share their problem from the previous session and how it was resolved in their mini-story.
● Then involve all the children in providing possible solutions to the problems on the board.
● Tell the children who have not completed their stories that now they should have lots of ideas of how to conclude their story.

Shared word-level work
● Tell the children that another important element of story is the setting. Ask the children to close their eyes to imagine what space would be like. What would they see and feel?
● Keeping their eyes closed, ask two children to describe what they are imagining. Capture their thoughts on the board, for example *dazzling stars, red-hot planets, empty black space, silence.*
● Advise the children to refer to the board to help them describe settings as they conclude their stories. Tell children who have concluded their stories to use the phrases to add a descriptive introduction to set the scene for their story.

Guided work
● Work with groups on their individual stories to support them in finding resolutions to problems and embellishing the story by describing the settings.

Differentiation

Less able
● With support, the children should conclude their story and focus on using some phrases from the board to describe the setting.

More able
● After paired discussion, ask the children to work individually to write a short descriptive introduction to their story that describes the setting.

Independent work
● Organise the children into their original 'settings' groups so that they can use their setting to play out a possible problem and resolution.
● Ask them to describe the scenes in their story, completing their story in this session.

Plenary
● Ask two children from the more able group to read out their setting descriptions.
● Also choose two children, including one from the less able group, to read their stories to the class.
● Conclude by telling the children that before displaying the stories on the wall they will be able to read them to younger children in the school, and arrange this.

Writing a blurb

Objectives

NLS
T7: To use titles, cover pages, pictures and blurbs to predict the content of unfamiliar stories.
S6: Through reading and writing, to reinforce knowledge of term *sentence* from previous terms.

What you need
● A selection of books that are new to the children, ideally of fantasy worlds.

Shared text-level work
● Tell the children that the fantasy world settings they have created provide a good idea of what the stories are going to be about. Say that book covers can do the same thing: by looking at the cover you can often work out what the story is about.
● Show the children the cover of a book from your selection and ask them to predict what the story might be about, using the title and image. Do this again with another book.
● Then show the children the blurb on the back of the first book and read it to see if they were correct. Repeat the process again.
● Help the children to make the connection that the blurb conveys the main problem in the story, but not what happens to resolve it.
● Ask the children if the blurbs made them want to read the stories.

Shared sentence-level work
● Ask the children what blurb they would write for their story about the spaceship engineer's line breaking. Demonstrate constructing an appropriate blurb in sentences. Discuss how questions are often included in blurbs to involve the reader in thinking about the story. For example:

> The engineer was working outside the ship when her line broke.
> Will the crew get her back in time?
> The crew of Spaceship 7 try to rescue their engineer who has lost contact with the ship.

● Draw attention once again to the blurb highlighting the problem that drives the story and giving an indication of setting and characters. Point out how the blurb doesn't fully reveal the story.

Guided work
● Work with two groups to support them writing blurbs for the stories they wrote in the first half of the unit.

Independent work
● Ask the children to create a blurb for their stories with the particular focus that as well as being exciting it should capture the fantasy world setting. Provide classroom assistant support and encourage discussion with the aim of making improvements.

Differentiation

Less able
● Ask the children to capture their stories as a drawing or painting for a cover page.

More able
● Ask the children to include in their blurbs a question related to the main problem in their story.

Plenary
● Ask the children to show their pictures and read their blurbs. Ask the other children if the blurbs would make them want to read the story. Compare them with the published books.
● Ask what they have learned about blurbs. What do they usually tell us? Do they reveal everything? What don't they tell us?
● Display the cover paintings and blurbs near the role-play areas.
● Discuss the differences between reviews and blurbs.

Literary critics

Objectives

NLS

T10: To compare and contrast preferences and common themes in stories.
W1: To learn the common spelling patterns for the long vowel phoneme *ie*.

S&L

11 Group discussion and interaction: To explain their views to others in a small group.

What you need

● A selection of fantasy stories you have been reading in story time.
● large sticky notes.

Shared text-level work

● Use the beginning of the session to celebrate the children's achievements in this topic: their fantasy world settings and the stories they have acted out and written, the display of cover pictures and blurbs, and their knowledge about problems and incidents that make stories exciting.

● Tell the children that in this session you are going to re-read some of the stories set in fantasy worlds that you have been reading in story time.

● Say that the focus is for them to say what it is about the story that they like so much.

● Ask the children to choose two of the fantasy stories you have read that they like best and encourage them to state their reasons for liking them, providing evidence from the text to support what they say. Elicit their responses by asking *What did you like about the main character/s? Was it a funny story and did you like the jokes? Did you think it was a scary story? Was it exciting? How would you describe the setting?* If you have a Big Book or are able to display the text, write the children's reasons on sticky notes and use them to label the appropriate parts of the text.

Shared word-level work

● Display the chart created in Hour 3 for different spelling patterns for the long *i* vowel sound.

● Discuss the collection, which should be quite extensive if children have been adding to it during this unit.

● Identify the most common spelling pattern and the rarest. Help the children to read and spell the uncommon ones.

Guided and independent work

● Organise for the children to work in groups of four. Provide each group with two familiar stories for them to discuss and explain reasons for preferences and dislikes.

● Remind the groups to take it in turns to express their views, to listen to each other's point of view and to back up their comments with reference to the texts.

● Emphasise that all opinions are valid and they do not have to agree on a favourite story.

Differentiation

Less able
● Lead and prompt the discussion where necessary.

More able
● Provide sticky notes so that children can label the evidence for their preferences and use them as reference in the plenary.

Plenary

● Organise for groups to explain their preferences to the class, referring to places in the text that substantiate their choices.

● Encourage the audience to ask the groups of children questions. This will promote dialogue between the children rather than the session being wholly teacher led.

● Conclude the unit by reinforcing all they have learned and how well-prepared they now are to write more stories. If there is time, suggest that the children write reviews of the story.

Patrick's class topic (1)

"**M**um, our class topic's on Space. Mrs Chapman says we're going to travel through space to distant planets and meet aliens and have adventures."

"Good," said Mum, "but now is not the time to go on about space, we have to hurry to get you to your swimming lesson."

All the way through Patrick's swimming lesson he couldn't stop thinking about Mrs Chapman's topic on outer space. He thought swimming must feel the same as flying so he imagined himself flying through the blackness of space, dodging meteors, diving away from asteroids...

"Patrick! What are you doing?" called his swimming teacher, "Keep up with the others, please!"

Patrick did try to keep up but every stroke was a stroke further away from a pursuing alien spacecraft. "Patrick, what are you doing?" called his swimming teacher again, causing Patrick to gasp and gulp. "It's time to finish, make your way to the side."

"Mum, I'd like to be an astronaut when I grow up and have adventures. Mrs Chapman says we're going to have adventures in our topic on outer space!"

"Good," said mum, "but now is not the time to go on about outer space, not when I'm driving Patrick, we have to hurry to get home for tea."

All the way through tea, Patrick steered his lamb chop spacecraft through pea meteorite showers and carrot asteroid attacks, searching for safety on potato planets.

"Patrick, what are you doing?" said his dad, "Eat your dinner properly, you're making such a mess!"

TERM 3

Patrick's class topic (2)

"Mum, what if we were invaded from outer space and aliens took over our house, and street, and everything?"

"Really!" said mum, "Now is not the time to talk about aliens, it's time for bed."

Patrick made his bed into a spaceship. He built up the pillows on either side and hung his blanket across the top. Then he snuggled up inside and said, "Goodnight Earth!"

"Patrick! It's time to get up."

"Oh no!" thought Patrick, "I've only just got in my spaceship."

"Mum," said Patrick, but he was immediately interrupted by mum saying, "Patrick, I really can't do with any more questions about aliens and outer space, I'm driving."

"Bye Patrick, have a good day!" Patrick didn't feel he would have a good day. He was fed up of never really getting into outer space.

In the classroom Mrs Chapman called the register. "What's the matter, Patrick? You look awfully miserable" she asked. Patrick sighed. "I know," said Mrs Chapman, "why don't you and Michelle go and explore the spaceship Mrs Walker has made for you in the activity bay."

"Really?" said Patrick.

"Really!" said Mrs Chapman.

Plot

■ Answer these questions to help you write your story plot.

1. Who leaves home?

_____

_____

2. Where do they go and what is it like?

_____

_____

3. What problem do they encounter?

_____

_____

4. How do they resolve it?

_____

_____

5. Does it end here?

_____

_____

6. How does it end?

_____

_____

Comparing stories

■ Compare stories using the subjects in this table.
Include your own fantasy world story.

Book title		
Author		
Setting		
Main characters		
What happens (include problem and how it is resolved)		
Illustrations		

■SCHOLASTIC

UNIT 2

Poetry 1

By following this unit children will enjoy poems with a seaside theme and patterned language. The suggested poems are lively and capture the many delightful images and impressions the seaside imprints on our memories. This is an ideal unit to inspire children's imagination and a natural precursor to the ten-hour non-fiction unit which begins on page 169. The skills the children learn in terms of reading poetry aloud and composing their own poetry would be best demonstrated in front of an audience; it is therefore suggested that you invite parents and carers to a performance of the poems as a finale to the unit. Hour 1 links to *Progression in Phonics*, Step 5.

Hour	Shared text-level work	Shared word-/ sentence-level work	Guided work	Independent work	Plenary
1 Fun words	Reading 'Let's do the flip-flop frolic!'; raising questions for understanding and interpretation.	Playing a dice game to change vowels to create new words.	Reading the poem at literal and inferential levels.	Continuing the dice game to generate tongue-twister rhymes.	Sharing lines and verses, playing again.
2 Reading to an audience	Reading with expression.	Interpreting the layout and grammar of the poem to assist reading with expression.	Reading the poem at literal and inferential levels.	Practising and supporting one another reading aloud.	Reading aloud to an audience.
3 Reading with expression	Introducing 'Sand'; practising reading aloud; discussing images in the poem.	Noting layout and punctuation to assist reading.	Reading the poem with understanding to assist expression.	Reading with expression leading to drawing a picture in response.	Discussing how their pictures and thoughts describe how they feel about the poem.
4 Seaside verses	Identifying the theme and key connective phrases to use as a model for writing.	Composing a short poem based on connective phrases and seaside words.	Composing a four-line poem using the connective phrases and seaside vocabulary.	Composing a four-line poem using the connective phrases and seaside vocabulary.	Reading verses aloud and evaluating them.
5 Thoughtful verses	Comparing drawings and verses; composing an additional verse that captures seaside imagery.	Comparing drawings and verses; composing an additional verse that captures seaside imagery.	Begin to assemble thoughts and words for composing a new verse for their poems.	Begin to assemble thoughts and words for composing a new verse for their poems.	Reading aloud completed verses, in preparation for an organised poetry event.

Key assessment opportunities
● Can the children read with appropriate pace, expression and emphasis?
● Do they notice common themes in poems?
● Can they write verses based on poems read?

Fun words

Shared text-level work
● Introduce 'Let's do the flip-flop frolic' from photocopiable page 167 and read it aloud.
● Emphasise the fun sounds of the words conveying the excitement and enjoyment of running down the beach for that first encounter with the sea.
● Point to the title, reading the words with the children. Tell the children the name of the poet (Judith Nicholls).
● Encourage volunteers to point to words for others to follow as that the poem is read aloud again.
● Ask questions to aid children's understanding of the poem. These can be at a literal level, for example *What words tell us that the poem is about the seaside? What words tell us it's about going into the sea?* Let children point to the words when answering.
● Other questions should help children to interpret the poem: *How do you feel when you go to the seaside? How do you know that's how the writer feels? Are there any words you can point to that make you feel excited?*

Shared word-level work
● Focus on the vocabulary of the poem. Say that you find it very difficult to say the first four lines. Ask the children to try saying the lines with their talk partners.
● Point out that the changing vowel sounds are causing the problems. Use the words *vowel* and *consonant* to talk about how changing the vowel is changing the word.
● Demonstrate rolling the three dice (in different colours to denote which should be rolled first) to create a new word.
● Write the word on the board and proceed to show how changing the vowel will produce a tongue twister as in the poem, for example *slom on a slim slam!* Involve the children so that several lines are created.

Guided and independent work
● Re-read the poem with a group. Ask questions that facilitate literal and inferential understanding as in the shared reading session.
● Organise the children to work in groups of four with a set of dice. Ask them to take turns to roll a dice each and one of them to write down the new word.
● All four should then collaborate to create a tongue twister line of poetry.
● Encourage the children to repeat this to create several fun lines.

Plenary
● Ask the groups to share their lines and verses.
● Have another quick game with the dice.
● Suggest that the children think of more tongue twisters, for example, using their names and hobbies.

UNIT 2 HOUR 2 ▮ Poetry 1

Reading to an audience

Objectives

NLS
T11: To participate in reading aloud.
S3: To read familiar texts aloud with pace and expression appropriate to the grammar.

S&L
9 Speaking: To interpret a text by reading aloud with some variety in pace and emphasis.
10 Listening: To express views about how a text has been presented.

What you need
● Photocopiable page 167
● a tape recording of you reading the poem.

Shared text-level work
● Display 'Let's do the flip-flop frolic!' and read it aloud together, focusing on reading with pace and expression.
● Invite children to read aloud individually, supporting them in their interpretation of what they are reading.
● Continue to use questions similar to those in Hour 1 to deepen understanding and interpretation of the text.
● Practise saying *flip flop frolic* with the children in order to encourage them to pronounce the words clearly.
● Try some other tongue twister such as *Peter Piper picked a peck of pickled peppers* and *She sells sea shells by the sea shore.*
● Give opportunities for pairs of children to practise saying the tongue twisters.
● Discuss the difficulties in pronouncing tongue twisters and how we can overcome those difficulties.

Shared sentence-level work
● Ask the children if there are things about the way the text is presented that offer clues about how it should be read.
● Confirm that there are and proceed to read the first four lines with no pauses – the children will be desperate to correct you!
● Ask the children what they think the dots mean after the word *and*, and why is *hop along* written in such small print? Why do the words grow from *hop along* to *dance along*?
● Practise saying the lines, getting louder and louder. What effect does the spacing have on the way you read *into–the*, and why are there more dots?
● Choose two children to read the poem again, taking these points into consideration, with appropriate pace, intonation and expression. Remind children that it is important to read poems expressively to retain the interest of the audience.

Guided and independent work
● For guided reading, continue as Hour 1, with a different group.
● Organise the children into groups of four and give each child a copy of the poem. Ask children to take turns to read the poem aloud while the others follow the text to provide support.
● Encourage the listeners to listen carefully and after the reading provide constructive comments, explaining their thoughts by reference to their understanding and interpretation of the text.

Differentiation

Less able
● Organise for the children to listen to the poem on tape while following the text.

More able
● Encourage the children to tape record their readings so that they can use the playback to note where improvements are needed.

Plenary
● Organise a formal space in the classroom for reading aloud. Place chairs around the area for the audience.
● Give the opportunity for at least one child from each group to read aloud in front of the audience.
● Allow children to try making up their own tongue twisters abljt the seaside topic or another topic of interest to them.

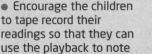 **163**

UNIT 2 HOUR 3 ◻ Poetry 1

Reading with expression

Objectives

NLS
T9: To read a variety of poems on similar themes.
T11: To participate in reading aloud.
S3: To read familiar texts aloud with pace and expression appropriate to the grammar.

What you need
● Photocopiable pages 167 and 168
● a tape recording of you reading 'Sand'.

Shared text-level work
● Read 'Sand' to the children for them to enjoy the fast pace that builds to a highly amusing finale.
● Practise reading the first verse together so that the children come to find it easy to read and can concentrate on reading it with pace.
● Discuss the images the poem conjures and relate them to the children's personal experiences of sand at the seaside.
● Talk about the fun of playing in the sand, the challenge of building sandcastles, of walking in deep soft sand, on hard damp sand nearer the sea, as well as the annoying things about sand getting everywhere!

Shared sentence-level work
● Ask the children what they notice about the first verse. What word is repeated? What words rhyme?
● Remind them of the first verse of 'Let's do the flip-flop frolic!' by displaying it alongside and pointing out the commas at the end of each line compared with the lack of commas in 'Sand'.
● Ask the children why they think John Foster hasn't used any commas and what effect this choice has on how we read the poem. (If necessary, remind them how *quickly* they can read the poem.)
● Ask the children what the exclamation mark means and what it tells you about how to read the line *Sand up your nose!* The exclamation mark should tell you to raise your voice with astonishment that you have *sand up your nose!*
● Now invite one or two children to read aloud the first verse of the poem.
● Tell them to apply their new understanding about how to read the verse so that they read with expression and pace.

Guided and independent work
● Work with two groups to read the poem, focusing on how the poem can be read expressively.
● Help them to appreciate that reading the poem appropriately can help them to understand and enjoy it better.
● Organise the children into groups of four where one of them (appointed by you) reads the poem aloud with expression.
● Following the reading, ask all of the children in each group to draw a picture that the poem has conjured for them.

Differentiation

Less able
● Let the children use the listening centre to hear you reading 'Sand' while they track the words on their texts.

More able
● Give the children the additional challenge of a written response.

Plenary
● Gather the children in a circle and discuss if their thoughts, pictures and written descriptions accurately describe how they feel about the poem.
● Compare and contrast images chosen for the pictures.
● Discuss the difference between prose and poetry – that poetry is separated onto different lines, should be read out rhythmically, and often (but not always) rhymes.

Seaside verses

Objectives

NLS
T10: To compare and contrast preferences and common themes in poems.
T15: To use poems or parts of poems as models for own writing.
W8: To learn new words from reading and shared experiences, and to make collections of words linked to particular topics.

What you need

● Photocopiable pages 167 and 168
● cards of connective words
● *Ketchup On Your Cornflakes?* by Nick Sharratt (Scholastic Hippo).

Shared text-level work

● Display 'Sand'. Read it for the children then read it aloud together.
● Lead the children in making a thematic connection between this poem and 'Let's do the flip-flop frolic!' – they are both about the seaside.
● If appropriate, remind the children of *Ketchup On Your Cornflakes?* by Nick Sharratt and notice how John Foster also uses *in your* and *on your* to unite two things, like *Sand in your sandwiches, Sand on your bananas.* Look at the other phrases John Foster uses in the poem to link things together (*between* and *up your*).

Shared word-level work

● Tell the children they are going to have a go at writing a similar poem.
● Ask them for ideas for a new verse. First decide on a 'seaside' word instead of *sand* by brainstorming some seaside words: *shrimps, buckets, ice-cream, sea, sunshine* and so on.
● List these on the board to start a collection of seaside words that the children can use and add to during this lesson and the next.
● Decide together on one of the words and construct a four-line verse around it using the connective phrases from John Foster's poem.
● At each stage, ask the children where the shrimps or ice-cream, for example, could be:

Shrimps in your beach bag
Shrimps up your nose
Shrimps in the sun cream
Shrimps between your toes.

Ice-cream in your sun hat
Ice-cream in your tea
Ice-cream on the deckchair
Ice-cream in the sea!

Guided and independent work

● Ask the children to work individually to compose a four-line verse as in the shared session. Remind them to choose a seaside word first and then think of four places it could be.
● Encourage them to draw on their own experiences of going to the seaside or of seaside-set stories or films.
● Provide preposition connective cards, *on, in, up, between, under* and so on, for the children to refer to.

Differentiation

Less able
● Support a group to make a collaborative poem.

More able
● Ask the children to write a collection of the seaside words they have used in their poem and add them to the class list.

Plenary

● Share the collaborative poem and one or two individual poems.
● Encourage listeners to explain and give reasons for their appreciation of the poems.

Thoughtful verses

Objectives

NLS
T9: To read a variety of poems on similar themes.
T16: To compose own poetic sentences, using repetitive patterns, carefully selected sentences and imagery.
W8: To learn new words from reading and shared experiences.

S&L
9 Speaking: To interpret a text by reading aloud with some variety in pace and emphasis.

What you need
● The children's pictures from Hour 3 and poems from Hour 4.

Shared text- and word-level work
● Consult the children whose pictures and verses you want to use and share.
● Display the chosen pictures and verses. Ask the children about the images captured in the picture and similar or different images captured in the verse.
● Ask questions related to how they feel, what it reminds them of and what it makes them think about. For example, when they see a sea shell what sounds can they hear when they hold it to their ear and what do the sounds remind them of? (Caves, mountains, roaring winds, raging seas and so on.)
● Do the same for the sand itself and ask the children to think about, for example, all the things that travel along the sand (feet, crabs claws, seagull's feet, donkeys' hooves). Another example might be eliciting memories of sandcastles.
● Continue to involve children in talking about their pictures and verses, supporting them in their explanations.
● Ask the children what more they would like to write and what words they would choose for another verse that says more about the picture connected with how they feel, what it reminds them of and what it makes them think about.
● Use one of the children's verses from the previous session as a starting point to construct another verse.
● Refer to the collection of words about the seaside for ideas for additional lines.
● As you write, ask questions such as *Does it sound right? Could we make it sound better? What picture does that conjure?*
● Tell the children that they are going to write additional verses to capture more of the feelings, fun, excitement, annoyance conveyed in their pictures.
● Motivate them further by telling them that the work they are doing is also in preparation for a poetry event to which their parents will be invited.

Guided and independent work
● Ask the children to add a verse to their verses from Hour 4, based on their pictures from Hour 3.
● Tell them not to be anxious about not completing their verse. Stress that it is more important to collect the words they want to use and *begin* to put them together, knowing that they can return to their composition in a later session.

Plenary
● Organise a formal space in the classroom for children in the higher ability group to read aloud their completed verses to the rest of the class Remind them to use plenty of expression when they read.
● Make time in later sessions for all the children to finish their poems, and organise the poetry reading.

Differentiation

Less able
● Provide sentence starters:
1. Reminds me of
2. Makes me feel
3. Makes me think of

More able
● Encourage the children to finish and practise performing their verses in preparation for the poetry event.

Let's do the flip-flop frolic!

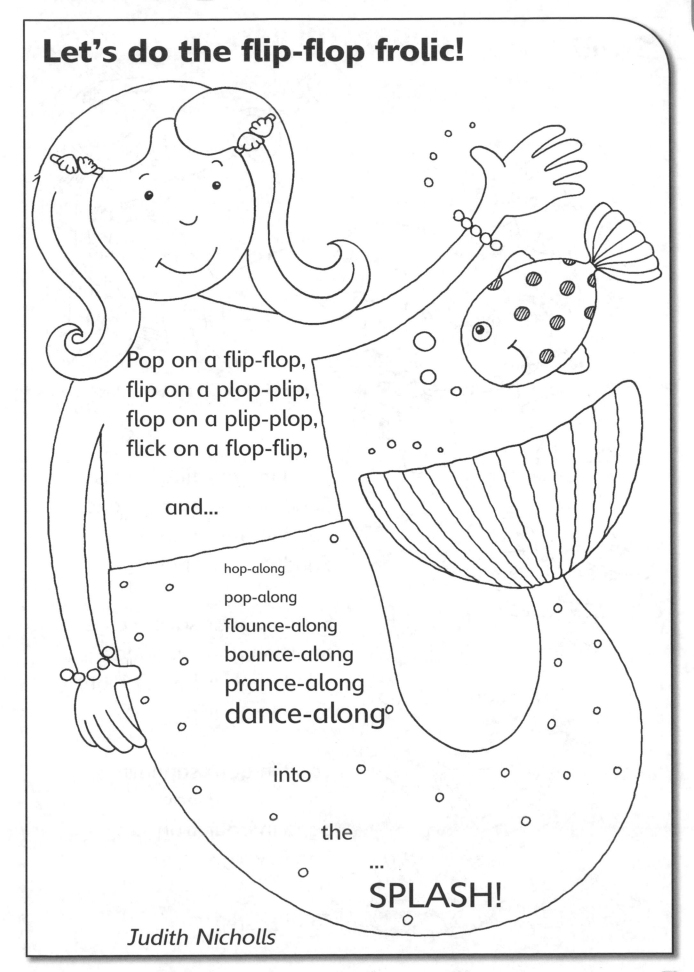

Pop on a flip-flop,
flip on a plop-plip,
flop on a plip-plop,
flick on a flop-flip,

and...

hop-along

pop-along

flounce-along

bounce-along

prance-along

dance-along

into

the

...

SPLASH!

Judith Nicholls

TERM 3

Sand

Sand in your fingernails
Sand between your toes
Sand in your earholes
Sand up your nose!

Sand in your sandwiches
Sand on your bananas
Sand in your bed at night
Sand in your pyjamas!

Sand in your sandals
Sand in your hair
Sand in your trousers
Sand everywhere!

John Foster

UNIT 3

Non-fiction 1 and 2

This unit would ideally follow a class visit to the seaside but can be adapted for other class visits such as to a local farm, city farm, park or market. The lessons cover both non-fiction units in the medium-term plan, resulting in class books and informative wall displays about the day out. The children will use digital cameras and computers and a range of non-fiction books. During the visit, use the digital camera to capture the sequence of events. Also take photographs of interesting creatures, plants and items found on the beach, and of seaside items in the beach shop. Also ensure to take photographs of individuals, pairs and groups of children involved in the various activities during the day. The unit covers the objectives of Unit 9 in *Developing Early Writing* and particularly lends itself to making cross-curricular links with art, geography and science, as well as with the unit on Poetry 1 (page 161).

Hour	Shared text-level work	Shared word-/ sentence-level work	Guided work	Independent work	Plenary
1 Photographs	Sequencing photographs of a class visit.	Spelling common irregular words.	Writing sentences to construct a recount.	Sequencing photographs, using single key words.	Talking about and listening to each other's sequence of events.
2 Class book and group books	Use sequence of photographs to begin constructing a recount for a class book.	Writing sentences for the recount.	Completing the class book.	Using their photograph sequence to make a group book of their visit.	Consolidate understanding about useful words to construct a recount.
3 Sequence words	Reading the new Big Book; recognising words that help to order events	Working on capitalisation for a book title.	Constructing a front cover for the Big Book.	Completing group books and making covers.	Reading each other's group books.
4 Captions	Writing captions for photographs.	Spelling new words, focusing on *-ing* words.	Writing a caption to a photograph on computer.	Writing a caption to a photograph on computer.	Printing photographs and accompanying captions for display.
5 Labels for sets	Discussing sets of objects and attaching labels to sets.	Writing labels.	Recalling topic words to use in writing labels for sets.	Sorting seaside objects into sets and attaching their own labels.	Looking at each other's sets and reading labels.

UNIT 3

Hour	Shared text level work	Shared word/ sentence level work	Guided work	Independent work	Plenary
6 Labels for objects	Writing labels for objects within the sets.	Writing labels for objects within the sets.	Labelling sets of pictures.	Labelling sets of pictures.	Playing game of spelling new words incorrectly for the children to correct.
7 Information books	Using non-fiction books for answering questions, with a focus on different ways information is represented.	Writing questions, using a question mark.	Examining different presentations in non-fiction texts.	Writing questions to be answered through later research.	Reinforcing the use of non-fiction books.
8 Questions and answers	Recording strategies for accessing information in non-fiction books.	Writing further questions.	Using strategies from whole-class work to find answers to their questions.	Using strategies from whole-class work to find answers to their questions.	Demonstrating how to use non-fiction books to answer questions; sharing some written answers.
9 Presenting information	Considering different ways of presenting information.	Reinforcing knowledge about the term sentence.	Answering questions through labelled pictures, captions and diagrams as appropriate.	Answering questions through labelled pictures, captions and diagrams as appropriate.	Talking about their reasons for representing their answers in a certain way.
10 A class display	Collecting key words for a photograph from given sentences.	Composing a caption for the photograph.	Writing a caption for their observational drawing from the information they have collected.	Writing a caption for their observational drawing from the information they have collected.	Celebrating achievements and learning.

Key assessment opportunities
● Have the children written about their visit?
● Can they locate information in non-fiction books to answer their own questions?
● Can they represent information in different ways?
● Do they use correct punctuation for writing sentences and questions?

Photographs

Objectives

NLS

T20: To write simple recounts linked to topics of study or to personal experience.

W7: To spell common irregular words from Appendix List 1.

S&L

11 Group discussion and interaction: To explain their views to others in a small group.

What you need

● Various photographs of the seaside visit.

Shared text-level work

● Tell the children that they are going to compile a class Big Book and group books about their recent visit. Recall what they did and saw.

● Organise the children into groups of four and give each group an enlarged photograph depicting a particular part of their day out.

● Tell them that you want them to talk about their photograph as a group first before they come together as a class to sort them into sequence to recount the events of the day.

● Allow the children two or three minutes to talk. Remind them to take turns and listen carefully to each other. Then move the children to form a circle, and place their photographs on the floor in front of them.

● Involve the children in talking about the sequence of events. Select children to stand and hold the pictures in order as you talk about them together.

● Emphasise and practise sequential vocabulary such as *first, then, after, when, next*, when ordering the photographs.

Shared word-level work

● Ask the children if they noticed some of the special words you used when putting the photographs in order (*first, next* and so on). Tell them that in order to write sentences for their books they will need to know how to spell these useful words.

● Take each word and demonstrate the 'Look, say, cover, write, check' method of learning spellings. Tell the children to *look* at the word on the board and offer suggestions about its pattern to aid memory. *Say* the word. Then *cover* it and ask children to *write* it on their own whiteboards from memory. Finally, ask the children to help you to *check* if they are correct.

Guided work

● Use the enlarged photographs from the shared session as a basis for sequencing and constructing sentences using the appropriate vocabulary of a recount, for example, *First we all got on the coach and set off on our journey to the seaside.*

Independent work

● Organise the children back in their groups of four. Give each group a set of smaller photographs and ask them to arrange the photographs in sequence along their tabletop.

● Provide strips of paper for them to write words such as those used in the shared session and, using paper clips, attach the words to the appropriate photograph.

● Encourage the children to work together to recall the visit, establish events in the photographs and discuss the order.

Differentiation

Less able

● Support and prompt the group discussion.

More able

● Ask the children to write sentences to clip to the photographs.

Plenary

● Place groups together so that each group can tell another group about their sequence of events.

📖 **171**

UNIT 3 HOUR 2 Non-fiction 1 and 2

Class book and group books

Objectives

NLS

T20: To write simple recounts linked to topics of study or to personal experience.
T12: Through shared and guided writing to apply phonological, graphic knowledge and sight vocabulary to spell words accurately.
S6: Through reading and writing to reinforce knowledge of term *sentence*.

What you need
● Photographs and labels from Hour 1
● a blank Big Book
● blank booklets for group books.

Shared text-level work
● Tell the children that in this session you are going to begin making a class book about their trip to the seaside and that they are also going to make group books from the sequences of photographs in Hour 1.
● Display the first photograph and sentence from the previous hour's guided writing session. Choose a child to point to the words as they are read and said.
● Then show the children the blank Big Book and attach the photograph on one side and the writing on the facing page.
● Do the same with the next photograph, again choosing a child to point and read and placing the photograph and writing on the next pages in the Big Book.
● Tell the children that they are going to use the photographs that they arranged in sequence in the previous session to make group books in the same way.

Shared sentence-level work
● Draw the children's attention to the way in which the words *First, Then, After, When, Next* and so on have been used to order the sentences so far.
● Use the next photograph to go in the Big Book as a starting point for constructing an appropriate sentence to follow on from the last one.
● Share your thinking about the writing, especially in choosing words that order events one after another.
● However, do use the children's own language to capture a more expressive recount than simply a technical one. Sentence beginnings such as *We thought, Sometimes, Often, We remembered* can evoke interesting embellishments.
● Remind the children of the 'Look, say, cover, write, check' routine for remembering spellings.

Guided work
● Continue composing the class book as in the shared session and complete it to use for shared reading in the next lesson.

Independent work
● Organise the children in the same groups of four as Hour 1. Provide each group with a blank book for arranging their sequence of photographs. Provide the children with suitably sized paper for them to write sentences that can be stuck in the book alongside the appropriate photograph.
● Advise them to work together and explain that they can finish in the next lesson if they run out of time.

Differentiation

Less able
● Ask a classroom assistant to scribe for the children where necessary.

More able
● Challenge the children to write additional sentences by drawing upon ideas in shared sentence work. Provide sentence beginnings on card.

Plenary
● Choose some well thought out sentences to further the children's understanding of the significance of the useful words that help order sentences.

Sequence words

Objectives

NLS
T18: To read recounts and begin to recognise generic structure, e.g. ordered sequence of events, use of words like *first, next, after, when.*
S5: To learn other common uses of capitalisation, e.g. for book titles.
W3: To read on sight other familiar words.

What you need
● The class Big Book
● the group booklets
● photographs of the visit.

Shared text- and word-level work
● Display the class Big Book and read it together by involving children in pointing and reading.
● Ask questions that lead the children in understanding the relevance of the sequence words.
● Begin by asking children what happened *before* or *after* one of the pictures. Then ask them what words tell us the order in which things happened in our book. Encourage children to say and point to these words.
● Re-read the book, asking the children to recall or predict the sequence word before you turn the page each time.

Shared sentence-level work
● Tell the children that they are going to need front covers and a title for the books they are making.
● Use the class Big Book to demonstrate the process of deciding upon a title and writing it using appropriate capitalisation.
● Ask the children to think of a variety of titles so that their group books have different names. Encourage them to talk about their ideas to each other as they do so.
● Take down the children's suggestions and write all of them on the board to model the use of capital letters, for example: *Kathryn, Alexandra, Kuda and Steven Go to the Seaside, Class 1's Hour at the Seaside.*
● Discuss with the children what sort of illustration, or which one of the photographs, would be a suitable cover image. Do they choose an eye-catching image?

Guided work
● Work with a group to construct a front cover page and title for the class Big Book.
● Ask them to discuss and agree on a photograph to include and how to lay it out with the title.

Independent work
● Encourage all of the groups to complete the sentences for their group book and then to create a bright and colourful front cover with a title and picture.
● Tell all the groups to brainstorm, share ideas fairly and come to a consensus. Make sure that everyone has a chance to participate that and no one dominates unfairly.

Differentiation

Less able
● Support the children in completing their books. Suggest simple, short titles where capitalisation is straightforward.

More able
● Encourage original ideas for titles and good use of capital letters.

Plenary
● Swap books between groups so that the children have the opportunity to read each other's recounts.
● Conclude the session by placing the Big Book and group books on a display bookshelf in the classroom for children to read at other times and use in other topic work.

Captions

Objectives

NLS
T12: Through shared and guided writing to apply phonological, graphic knowledge and sight vocabulary to spell words accurately.
T21: To use the language and features of non-fiction texts, e.g. captions for pictures.
W6: To investigate and learn spellings of verbs with *ing* endings.
W8: To learn new words from shared experiences.

What you need
● Photographs of the visit.

Shared text-level work
● Tell the children that in this session they are going to write captions for photographs of themselves and their friends to set up a gallery in the classroom of their visit to the seaside.
● Discuss what a gallery is. Then ask the children if they have heard the word *caption* before and what they think it means. Establish that a caption is a short piece of writing that accompanies a picture and gives a little bit of information about it.
● Display a photograph (using an interactive whiteboard if possible) and tell the children that you need their help in writing a caption that briefly explains the picture. Take ideas and prompt the use of the children's names, for example:

> Kathryn collecting shells
> Jamal writing his name in the sand
> Phoebe and David eating ice-creams.

● Do this for several pictures and involve the children in composing simple phrases whilst you display the writing process on the screen. Demonstrate that the captions are short and simple and are saying what is happening. If appropriate, explain that they don't need to be full sentences.

Shared word-level work
● Continue the session by asking the children to discuss with their talk partners all the new words they have been using when talking about their day at the seaside, such as the ones they have just used for the captions.
● Draw attention to the *-ing* endings of the action words: *collecting, writing, eating* and so on. Ask the children to suggest other action words ending in *-ing* and write them on the board. Involve the children in the spelling.
● Investigate what happens to a word when adding *-ing*. Encourage the children to find the 'rule' each time: leaving it the same, doubling the last letter or omitting the *e*.

Guided and independent work
● Organise the children to work in pairs at a computer. Prepare the file so that an appropriate photograph of themselves, either alone or with classmates, is on screen.
● Ask them to recall what they were doing in the picture and to type an accompanying caption.
● Children will require support for this activity, so both you and the classroom assistant should help. If possible ask parents to give additional support, ideally those who accompanied the children on the visit.

Differentiation

Less able
● Help the children with verb endings and the word order of the captions.

More able
● Encourage the children to spell check their work.

Plenary
● Show the children how to print their own photographs and captions which can then be displayed in the visit gallery.

UNIT 3 HOUR 5 ⬜ Non-fiction 1 and 2

Labels for sets

Objectives

NLS

T12: Through shared and guided writing to apply phonological, graphic knowledge and sight vocabulary to spell words accurately.

T21: To use the language and features of non-fiction texts, e.g. labelled diagrams.

W10: To practise handwriting in conjunction with spelling and independent writing.

What you need
● Collections of objects and photographs of objects from the visit
● hoops
● string
● cards for labels.

Differentiation

Less able
● See Guided and independent work.

More able
● Encourage the children to type and print out their labels, experimenting with fonts and type size.

Shared text-level work
● Before the lesson, prepare a floor display in the carpet area of different items collected at the seaside and photographs of items seen there.
● Tell the children that in this session they are going to work in groups to make labelled collections of the things they brought back and saw at the seaside.
● Organise the children to sit with their talk partners in a circle around the floor display.
● Ask the children to identify each object, then help them to sort them into sets using the children's own criteria. These criteria could be, for example, *What we saw in the rock pools, What we found in the sand, What we bought in the beach shop.* Provide hoops to demarcate the sets.
● Provide plenty of opportunity for children to talk with their partners to thoroughly discuss the choices being made.
● Tell the children that you want to label the sets and look around the room to read other examples of labels.
● Point out that labels are usually only one or two words (not descriptive phrases or sentences as in captions).

Shared word-level work
● As the children decide on labels for the sets (this will depend on their chosen criteria), involve them in shared writing for correct spelling.
● Make a point of involving the children in attaching the labels to the hoops using string, as this helps to denote a label rather than a caption.

Guided work
● Work with a lower ability group to recall the topic words they have been learning and using so far in this unit. Make a list of these together and use them to write clear labels.

Independent work
● Organise for groups of four to work around a table or on a floor space containing another assortment of seaside items and photographs. Ask the children to sort the items into a maximum of three sets, again using their own criteria.
● Ask them to agree and write labels and check their spellings, before attaching the labels to the hoops using lengths of string.

Plenary
● Organise for the groups to travel around the classroom to see each other's sets and read their labels.
● Ensure that some of the work contributes to a display in the classroom, along with the class recount photo-books and captioned photographs.
● Also make a link to art by complementing the display with observational drawings where possible (see Hour 7).

UNIT 3 HOUR 6 📖 Non-fiction 1 and 2

Labels for objects

Objectives

NLS

T12: To apply phonological, graphic knowledge and sight vocabulary to spell words accurately.
T21: To use the language and features of non-fiction texts, e.g. labelled diagrams.
W8: To learn new words from reading and shared experiences.

What you need
● Display of sets from Hour 5
● string
● cards for labels
● photocopiable pages 181 and 182.

Shared text- and word-level work
● Use a display of a group of sets created in the previous session as a starting point for this session.
● Arrange the sets on the floor with their labels and organise the children to sit in a circle around them.
● Involve the children in reading the labels.
● Now tell the children that you want to label the individual items within the sets.
● Ask the children to identify some of the objects in each of the sets, and to consider what labels they could make for the individual items.
● Ask a child to choose and hold an object from a certain set, for example, a spade or bucket from a set of *Tools* or *Things we took with us*, and ask the other children how they could label it (by its name or by its colour and size, for instance).
● Take some of the children's suggestions and demonstrate making card labels for the objects and photographs, for example, a blue bucket, a long-handled spade, a digital camera and a fishing net.
● Involve the children in writing labels for other objects.
● Give individual children lengths of string and ask them to connect the object to the label.
● Demonstrate different strategies for spelling new words and reinforce the need for children to apply the same strategies in their group activities.

Guided and independent work
● Show the children photocopiable pages 181 and 182 and read the labels of the sets together.
● Then ask the children to work individually to identify and label the pictures.
● Give support where necessary, and encourage the children to use information from the display as appropriate.
● If they have time, encourage the children to draw and label any objects they think are missing from the sets.

Plenary
● Play a game of spelling some of the key topic words (such as *shells, crab, bucket, spade*) incorrectly and encourage the children to correct you.
● Discuss the 3-D labelled display and position it so that children can add to it at other times.
● Ask the children to explain some of the strategies they are using to spell words, for example, by drawing on knowledge of spelling patterns for long vowel sounds, by segmenting clusters into phenomes, by drawing on knowledge of common spelling patterns and words within words.
● Discuss the 3-D labelled display and position it so that the children can add to it at other times.

Differentiation

Less able
● Involve the children in completing the labels in the shared session.

More able
● Encourage the children to draw and label their own set, using a similar layout to the photocopiable sheets.

Information books

Objectives

NLS

T17: To recognise that non-fiction books on similar themes can give different information and present similar information in different ways.

T22: To write own questions prior to reading for information.

S7: To add question marks to questions.

S3: To read aloud with pace and expression appropriate to the grammar, e.g. pausing at full stops, raising voice for questions.

What you need

● Shells collected from the visit

● non-fiction books on the seaside, sea life, shells and so on

● tape recorders.

Differentiation

Less able

● Ask the children to record their questions on tape.

More able

● Ask the children to use the non-fiction books on display to begin answering their questions.

Shared text-level work

● Link the focus on shells and seashore life in the following three sessions to art so that children each produce an observational drawing for a wall display.

● Prepare a floor display of shells in order to demonstrate how to find out about them using the non-fiction books.

● Organise the children to sit with their talk partners in a circle around the display. Begin by asking pairs of children to select a shell. Allow time for them to handle and examine the shell and talk about it together. Establish that it would be good to find out more about their shell, such as what lived in it, and discuss the questions they might ask.

● Introduce the collection of books and involve the children in selecting suitable books for finding out about shells from looking at cover pictures and titles.

● Focus on two books that present similar information about a shell in different ways, for example pictures/photographs, labels, captions, diagrams. Help the children to see that much of the information is the same. Can they find out more from one than the other?

● Reinforce children's knowledge about using information books by flicking through pages to notice pictures, captions and headings, rather than starting at the beginning as when reading a story.

● Encourage them to make use of indexes and contents too.

Shared sentence-level work

● Use one of the children's questions to demonstrate writing a question. For example, if they want to find out *what* lives inside a shell involving the children in transposing to put *what* at the beginning of the sentence.

● Take the opportunity to talk about other useful question words such as *where, when* and *how*.

● Continue to write the sentence but pretend to forget to put the question mark at the end to encourage the children's involvement.

Guided work

● Look at some of the books again, drawing attention to the different ways information is represented and different methods of finding information quickly.

Independent work

● Organise for talk partners to work together to write a selection of questions related to their shell to use in a 'finding out' activity in the next lesson.

● Remind them to use a capital letter at the beginning and question mark at the end.

Plenary

● Reinforce how to use non-fiction books by asking pairs from the higher ability group to explain what they have done.

UNIT 3 HOUR 8 Non-fiction 1 and 2

Questions and answers

Objectives

NLS

T17: To recognise that non-fiction books on similar themes can give different information and present similar information in different ways.

T19: To identify simple questions and use text to find answers. To locate parts of text that give particular information including labelled diagrams and charts.

T22: To write own questions prior to reading for information and to record answers.

What you need

● Non-fiction books on the seaside.

Shared text-level work

● Use this part of the session to reinforce how to use non-fiction books to find out information as well as demonstrating that similar information can be presented in many different ways.

● Show the children your selection of books on the seaside.

● Begin by establishing one of the children's questions from the previous session as a starting point for finding out. Display the question and read it together.

● Involve the children in using the non-fiction books to find out information and write on the board (so that it can be displayed for reference during the session) the strategies being used. Strategies might include:

> ● not starting at the beginning
> ● looking for appropriate pictures
> ● scanning headings and titles
> ● referring to the index and contents
> ● reading captions, labels, diagrams and charts.

● Ask the children to choose a suitable book for answering the question and to tell you how to find the answer.

Shared sentence-level work

● Ask the children if there are any more questions that they would like to ask on this particular subject and reinforce how to write questions.

● Remind the children that a question mark is needed at the end of the sentence.

Guided and independent work

● Prepare tables with appropriate selections of non-fiction books about the seashore for the children to refer to. There should be no more than six children at each table.

● Give the children their written questions from Hour 7 to answer using the books on the table.

● Refer them to the techniques on the board and give help with difficult vocabulary as necessary.

● Answers need only be oral at this stage, so ask the pairs to tell each other what information they have found.

Differentiation

Less able
● Ask the children to tape record their answers.

More able
● Encourage the children to begin writing the answers they have rehearsed orally.

Plenary

● Invite pairs of children to demonstrate how they have used non-fiction books to answer their questions.

● Ask the children if all their questions have been answered.

● If not, invite suggestions of a book from a different table that might be suitable, as not all the books necessarily have all the same information.

● Conclude by inviting a child to show how he or she could write an answer to his or her question in the form of a sentence.

Presenting information

Objectives

NLS
T21: To use the language and features of non-fiction texts, e.g. labelled diagrams, captions for pictures.
S6: Through reading and writing to reinforce knowledge of term *sentence*.

What you need

● Non-fiction books on the seaside
● the children's work from Hour 8.

Shared text-level work

● Use an example of a child's question and initial written answer from the previous session to reinforce the process of finding out information using non-fiction books.
● Ask the child if he or she would like to provide the answer in a different way, such as a labelled picture or diagram similar to those found in the books.
● Involve all the children in thinking about how information is displayed in the books and decide how best to present the child's written response. Would it be better as a labelled picture? Or a caption to a picture? Would a detailed diagram be appropriate? For example:

● If the question asked is *Where do sea anemones live?* with the answer *Sea anemones live in rock pools on the seashore*, this could be represented with a photograph or picture of a rock pool with labels to rocks and seaweed and to the sea anemone.

● If the question is *Where do you find rock pools?* with the answer *Rock pools are found on the seashore*, then a photograph of the seashore with rock pools and an appropriate caption could represent this.

● If the question is *Why are there worm casts on the sand?* with the answer *Worm casts are from worms buried under the sand*, this might be best represented by a diagram showing in section the worm buried in the sand in a 'u'-shape with the cast on the surface.

Shared sentence-level work

● Choose another question to discuss, drawing upon a variety of presentation methods.
● Reinforce the term *sentence* by involving the children in discussion about whether one word labels are sentences. Ask the children what grammatical features denote a sentence. If the sentence were made into a labelled picture, what key words would be retained?

Guided and independent work

● Using the same group organisation and resources as the previous session, tell the children to represent their answers in an appropriate diagram, labelled picture or caption for a picture, as discussed in the shared session.
● Encourage the children to discuss their ideas and use the non-fiction books for ideas on how to represent different types of information and give answers to questions.

Differentiation

Less able
● Aid discussion to help the children make decisions about representing their answers.

More able
● If the children are writing a sentence, ask them to check it is punctuated correctly and makes grammatical sense.

Plenary

● Invite the children to talk about the decisions they made to best represent the information they found. Ask why a label was more appropriate than a caption, or why a diagram might be better, reinforcing the shared text-level work.
● Display the work with the Big Book and recount booklets.

UNIT 3 HOUR 10 Non-fiction 1 and 2

A class display

Objectives

NLS
T19: To locate parts of the text that give particular information.
T21: To use the language and features of non-fiction texts, e.g. captions for pictures.
S6: Through reading and writing to reinforce understanding of term *sentence*.

What you need
● Non-fiction books on the seaside
● photocopiable page 183.

Shared text-level work
● Say to the children that they are going to provide captions for their observational drawings to add to the display.
● Tell them that they will be using the information they have collected throughout the unit.
● Display photocopiable page 183.
● Say to the children that someone has found out lots of information about crabs and involve the children in reading the snippets of information.
● Help the children with any difficult words, but encourage them to join in as you re-read.
● Encourage anyone who has been studying crabs to offer any other interesting information and write it on the board.
● Ask the children how they could make a caption or captions for the picture by selecting key words and phrases from the sentences on the sheet.
● Encourage them to talk about why they want to include some information and leave some out.
● Collect key words on the board.

Shared sentence-level work
● Compose a caption from the key words, phrases and sentences displayed.
● For example, the two sentences *Crabs have a pair of pincers to pinch your toes* and *One pincer is bigger than the other… to defend itself* could lead to the caption *Watch out for those pincers!*
● Draw attention to the appropriate punctuation.

Guided and independent work
● Using all the appropriate information they collected in previous sessions, ask the children to work individually to write a caption to accompany their observational drawing.
● Encourage them to make use of the non-fiction books and the photocopiable sheet to guide their writing.
● Provide support for any children who are struggling to collate their information or pick out the most interesting or most suitable key information to use.

Differentiation

Less able
● Scribe for the children if necessary, but encourage them to try out one or two captions orally.

More able
● Encourage the children to provide more than one caption or a longer caption of more than one sentence.

Plenary
● Use this time to celebrate the children's achievements and the learning that has taken place.
● Organise the children to sit on chairs facing the materials they have produced as a result of this project: class Big Book, group books, labelled sets and objects, observational drawings. The classroom should be full of their work!
● Conclude by involving the children in reading their captions from this session and temporarily pin some to the appropriate drawing in readiness for completing the display.

Things we bought at the beach shop

TERM 3

Things we saw on the beach

Crabs

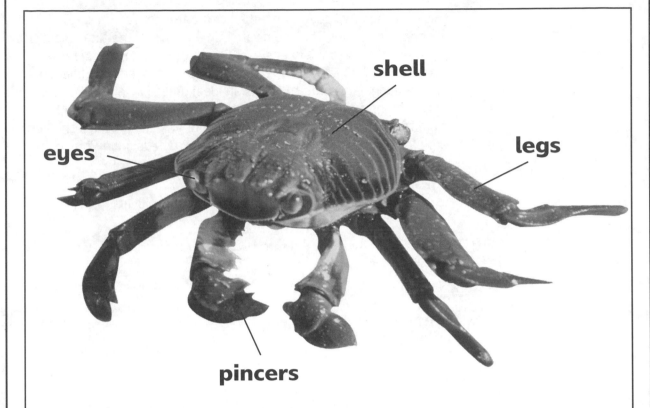

shell

eyes

legs

pincers

◀ Write a caption.

Crabs have 10 legs.

We can eat crabs. They are delicious!

Hermit crabs live in the empty shells of other creatures.

Crabs have a pair of pincers to pinch your toes!

One pincer is often bigger than the other to grab and hold tiny creatures it wants to eat and to defend itself.

Crabs shelter in rock pools and underneath seaweed.

Crabs scuttle sideways.

Have you seen a crab rocking back on its hind legs and waving its pincers at you?

UNIT 4

Poetry 2

This unit uses two poems on a theme of outer space, offering links to science and history. The poems are quite different; the first, 'Blast Off!', captures both the anxiety and excitement of preparing to meet unknown worlds, whereas the second, 'Aliens', provides a wilder and funnier imaginary context. This is an ideal unit to inspire children's imaginations and is a natural precursor to 'Narrative 1', page 145. Dramatisation and role-play form the major vehicle by which children explore the poems. Hours 3 to 5 link with *Progression in Phonics*, Step 7.

Hour	Shared text-level work	Shared word-/ sentence-level work	Guided work	Independent work	Plenary
1 Blast Off!	Reading and sharing responses to the poem.	Picking out key words; spelling new words.	Reading aloud with expression.	Making a thought bubble picture, putting themselves in the poem.	Explaining what astronauts might think before taking off.
2 Appreciation of reading aloud	Practise reading with expression, gesture and volume.	Discussing what they liked about their partner's reading of their poem.	Reading aloud with expression.	Reading poem aloud and discussing how well it was read.	Reporting back on performances.
3 Our rhymes	Substituting words to make new poems.	Creating spelling chart for long vowel sounds *oe* and *ai*.	Writing a new collaborative poem.	Creating new funny poems based on the model from shared work.	Enjoying the new poems.
4 Imagine an alien	Drawing the alien from a reading of the poem.	Playing a game to identify vowel phonemes.	Interpreting text to develop expression.	Creating picture of another alien with oral descriptions.	Talking about their alien creating; choosing key descriptions from the tape recording.
5 Our poetry	Reading with expression; composing poetic sentences.	Identifying spelling patterns for *ee* sound.	Composing a verse of sentences.	Composing poetic sentences describing their aliens.	Appreciation of poetic sentences and paintings.

Key assessment opportunities
● Can the children interpret contexts to assist reading for meaning?
● Can they read expressively and talk about how well others read aloud?
● Do they apply knowledge of long-vowel spelling patterns to their own writing?

Blast Off!

Objectives

NLS
T2: To use contextual knowledge to make sense of what they read.
T9: To read a variety of poems on similar themes.
W8: To learn new words from reading and shared experience, and to make collections of words linked to particular topics.

What you need

● Role-play area that is the inside of a spaceship, including control panel, porthole windows, space suits and helmets
● photocopiable page 190.

Shared text-level work

● Display the poem 'Bast off!' from photocopiable page 190 and read it to the children with suitable expression.
● Following the reading, ask questions about the poem to establish what it is about. For example:

> ● Why are there numbers counting backwards?
> ● What do you think is happening?
> ● What parts of the poem tell you what is happening?
> ● How do you know it's about a rocket?

● Ask further questions that enable children to imagine what it is like to be in a spaceship about to take off. Ask what they might be thinking if they were about to blast off on a voyage into space:

> ● What words tell you how the astronaut is feeling?
> ● How would you feel?
> ● Would you miss your family and friends?
> ● Would you feel excited about travelling to unknown places?

● Write some of the children's responses on the board in a thought bubble to prepare children for their tasks.

Shared word-level work

● Choose children to pick out and point to words and phrases in the poem that make pictures in the mind, such as *outer space, weird aliens.*
● Say to the children that, although we know the poem is about a *spaceship* and *astronauts*, those words don't appear in the poem.
● Involve the children in trying to spell the words *spaceship* and *astronaut.*
● Ask the children what other words they know about outer space and spaceships. Involve the children in spelling the words they suggest. Display the word collection for reference during this and further sessions in the unit.

Guided work

● Read with a group to develop the children's skills of reading aloud with expression.

Independent work

● Organise the children to work in pairs. Tell them to imagine they are two astronauts in a spaceship about to take off for outer space. Ask them to draw a picture of themselves inside the spaceship and to use thought bubbles containing text or additional pictures.

Differentiation

Less able
● Organise for this group to play in the role-play area using the spaceship to take them to imaginary worlds.

More able
● Ask the children to be prepared to explain their pictures in the plenary.

Plenary

● Ask more able children to show and explain their pictures, in particular the things they were thinking before take off.

185

TERM 3

Objectives

NLS
T11: To participate in reading aloud. **S3:** To read familiar texts aloud with pace and expression appropriate to the grammar.

S&L
9 Speaking: To interpret a text by reading aloud with some variety in pace and emphasis.
12 Drama: To discuss why they like a performance.

What you need
● Photocopiable page 190
● recording of the poem on tape.

Appreciation of reading aloud

Shared text-level work
● Read the poem with a flat tone, and too quickly or too slowly, and mumble or don't articulate some words. Ask the children what is wrong with your reading.
● Then read it again, this time in a way that takes the children's suggestions into account and so that the children can clearly hear the build up of tension as the countdown proceeds towards blast off.
● Try to capture the hesitancy in *the space that lies ahead*, the sadness in *the years we'll be away*, the reflectiveness in *look back upon this day* so that the children can gather a deeper understanding of the poem.

Shared sentence-level work
● Clear a space for the children to stand together in pairs or sit on chairs comfortably to practise reading aloud.
● Provide copies of the poem for each pair so that the children can quietly practise reading the poem aloud to one another, emphasising the importance of expression, using variation in tone and subtle gesture as you did.
● Encourage the pairs to share ideas and evaluate each other's reading, giving positive comments.
● Invite the children to talk to the class about the effective features of their partners' reading, for example how well they used different voices, pace and gesture. Did they speak clearly and expressively?

Guided work
● Work with another group to re-read the poem with expression. Encourage them to develop their performance in light of the class discussion if appropriate.

Independent work
● Organise the pairs into groups of four. Ask them to take turns where one pair reads the poem aloud whilst the other two listen and provide useful comments about clarity, pace, voice, gesture and expression.

Differentiation

Less able
● Provide a listening centre for children to read the poem as they hear it.
● Then in pairs ask them to practise reading aloud, taking turns at reading the numbers then the words.

More able
● Encourage children to learn the poem by heart to free up their performance skills.

Plenary
● Select pairs of children to report on their group partners' performances.
● Use the following questionto encourage children to talk positively about other's performances:

> ● What particular bit of the poem was read really well?
> ● Can you explain why it sounded so good?
> ● Have you any suggestions for making changes to the reading?
> ● Are there parts that should be read more softly/quickly/thoughtfully/fearfully/confidently/excitedly?

UNIT 4 HOUR 3 Poetry 2

Our rhymes

Objectives

NLS
T15: To use poems as models for own writing, e.g. by substituting words or elaborating on the text.
W1: To explore common spelling patterns for long vowel phonemes: *ai, oo.*

What you need
● Photocopiable page 190
● even-numbered lines from photocopiable page 190 on strips of card
● tape recorders.

Shared text-level work
● Use this re-reading to focus on the rhymes in the poem.
● Display the poem and read the first line, but instead of reading the second line substitute *9 Do be quick don't be ___*, gesturing to the children to supply the rhyming word (*slow*).
● Do the same for the other lines, for example:

> 8 the space that lies ahead
> 7 No thanks, I'll stay in ___ (bed)
> 6 the years we'll be away
> 5 a game I'd rather ___ (play)
> 4 set off to outer space'
> 3 hurry up and wash your ___ (face).

● Tell the children that they are going to think and write alternative rhyming lines in their activities – the funnier the better!

Shared word-level work
● Say to the children that to write rhyming lines they will need to think of lots of rhyming words. Begin by asking them to think of words that rhyme with *go* and *slow*. Focus on the spelling patterns and begin a spelling chart, for example:

slow	no	though	sew	toe	goat
crow	go				coat
snow					

● Explore spelling patterns for the long *a* sound in *away* and *space* and begin another chart for the children to refer to:

away	walt	space	stralght
day	bait	face	
stray		lane	
		cane	
		gate	

Guided work
● Work with groups to support the composition of rhyming lines. Brainstorm ideas to produce a collaborative poem.

Independent work
● Provide pairs of children with the even-numbered lines from the poem and ask them to compose rhyming lines to create a new and funny poem.
● Remind the children to maintain the space theme and refer to the rhyme charts constructed earlier in the hour.

Plenary
● Select children to read their poems aloud. Enjoy the funny rhymes.

Differentiation

Less able
● Ask poor writers to use hand held tape recorders to record their rhyming lines.

More able
● Challenge the children to provide more than one rhyming line each time, then try them out in the poem in order to choose their favourite.

UNIT 4 HOUR 4 📖 Poetry 2

Imagine an alien

Objectives

NLS

T16: To compose own poetic sentences, using imagery.

W1: To segment words into phonemes for spelling.

What you need
● Photocopiable page 191
● an 'Alien' outline made by drawing around a child on wallpaper/lining paper
● painting equipment
● tape recorder.

Shared text-level work
● Pin the 'alien' outline to the wall as the basis for making the alien in the poem.
● Display the poem and read it aloud with lots of stresses and exaggerated expression.
● Establish what it is about, then move quickly to focus on what the alien looks like.
● Go through the poem line by line. At the end of each line invite a child to draw the description onto the life-size outline, so creating a picture of the alien. (Use large coloured felt tips for a vivid picture.)
● Stand back and admire the alien. Ask the children if it scares them and would frighten them if they saw a real one!

Shared word-level work
● Recap some of the different spellings found for the long vowel sound *a*, by referring to the spelling chart from Hour 3. Make a new column for stand-alone *a* spelling pattern as in *alien*. (Though there are very few words like this.)
● Segment some of the words in the chart by their phonemes.
● Play the game of placing sound dots underneath the words, for example:

p a c e	f a c e	p a i n	p l a t e	r a i n
* * *	* * *	* * *	* * * *	* * *
c r a t e	s t a i n	c h a s e	c h a i n	
* * * *	* * * *	* * *	* * *	

Guided work
● Re-read the poem with a focus on interpreting the text to develop expression and intonation.
● To enable all children to paint a picture, take out small groups from independent work to for approximately ten minutes each, thus allowing ten minutes for painting.

Independent work
● Ask the children to create a picture of an imaginary alien *different* from the one in the poem and to talk about their choices and inspiration.
● If possible, use a tape recorder to capture some of the children's oral descriptions as they chat about their work. (Use art lessons for completing the pictures.)

Differentiation

Less able
● Organise for the group to work together to create a life-size alien, with adult support.

More able
● Encourage more confident speakers to ask questions and instigate conversations during the painting work.

Plenary
● Select two or three children to show and talk about their picture.
● Play back the tape so that the children can hear the ideas they had while working.
● Pick out descriptive and lively words and phrases from the tape that could be used in a poem. Write the words on the board for use in the next session.

UNIT 4 HOUR 5 Poetry 2

Objectives

NLS
T16: To compose own poetic sentences.
S6: To reinforce knowledge of term *sentence*.
W1: To identify phonemes in speech and writing.
W5: To recognise words by common spelling patterns.

What you need
● Photocopiable page 191
● the children's artwork from Hour 4.

Our poetry

Shared text-level work
● Remind the children of the poem 'Alien!' by reading it aloud. Invite children to use the pointer so that they are pointing to words read.
● Then encourage them to read the poem with expression, gesture and appropriate volume and pace.
● Refer to the word bank of descriptive/action packed words collected in the previous session. Involve the children in choosing phrases to put together to make poetic sentences full of imagery. For example, put together words and phrases such as *goggly eyes, eyes on stalks, revolving eyes* into a sentence: *The alien had goggly revolving eyes on stalks.* Demonstrate the composition process by selecting words that create the best picture.
● Tell the children that they are going to compose their own poetic sentences for the aliens they have created.

Shared word-level work
● Tell the children that they are going to make a new spelling chart to help them spell words containing the sound *ee* as in *teeth*. Choose a child to find and point to the word *teeth* in the poem.
● Read the next verse together and ask the children if they can hear the *ee* sound again (in *creature* and *eat*).
● Ask the children what they notice about the *ee* spelling in *teeth* and the *ea* spelling in *creature* and *eat*. Start a spelling chart for the long *e* sound similar to those established in previous sessions for children to add to.

Guided work
● Work with a group to compose poetic sentences about their aliens by supporting them in selecting and inventing descriptive words and phrases.
● Compose a number of sentences to make a poetic 'verse'. Suggest that children try to make complex sentences by using connectives.

Independent work
● Place drawings and paintings at the children's places so that they can use them for further inspiration during the session.
● Tell them to compose a sentence that conjures a picture of their alien like the one you composed in the shared text session. Ideally, they should attempt to write more than one sentence. Provide suitably sized paper – strips or A5 sheets.

Plenary
● Organise the children to sit in a circle. Ask two or three to read their poetic sentences, encouraging them to read with expression.
● Invite other children to say why they liked the poetic sentences and the reading.
● Arrange the paintings and the accompanying lines of poetry as a class display.

Differentiation

Less able
● Working collaboratively, and with classroom assistant support, the group should attempt some descriptive, action-packed sentences about their alien.

More able
● Ask the children to compose more then one sentence to make a short poem.

Blast Off!

10

Control say "you're clear to go"

9

"O.K. then make it so!"

8

the space that lies ahead

7

where man has yet to tread

6

the years we'll be away

5

look back upon this day

4

set off to outer space

3

the dangers yet to face

2

weird aliens and strange planets

1

but no time left – it's

BLAST OFF!

Kathleen Taylor

Alien!

Wobbly jobbly horrible thing!
Knuckles decked in cygnet rings
Some were fingers, some were toes,
He even had one up his nose!

Spikey bony pointed head,
All ten eyes sparkling red,
Pokey tongue and pokey ears,
Nasty teeth as sharp as spears.

Warty spotty slimy creature
Looked around and said "I'll eat ya!"
Nasty words and nasty notions,
Now's the time for magic potions!

The captain cried "I've got a spell!"
I hope it works, but time will tell.
Take five frogs legs and two bats' ears,
Twirl them round 'til he disappears.

Kathleen Taylor

In this series:

ISBN 0-439-97164-0
ISBN 978-0439-97164-5

ISBN 0-439-97165-9
ISBN 978-0439-97165-2

ISBN 0-439-97166-7
ISBN 978-0439-97166-9

Available September 2005:

ISBN 0-439-97167-5
ISBN 978-0439-97167-6

ISBN 0-439-97168-3
ISBN 978-0439-97168-3

ISBN 0-439-97169-1
ISBN 978-0439-97169-0

ISBN 0-439-97170-5
ISBN 978-0439-97170-6

To find out more, call: 0845 603 9091
or visit our website www.scholastic.co.uk